The 7 Essential Habits of Wealthy Real Estate Investors

---

10 Years, 4 Million Equity

24,000 Net Per Month!

WHY NOT YOU?

Joseph Neilson, The Real Estate Professor

Copyright © 2014 Joseph Neilson
All rights reserved.
ISBN:1506179533
ISBN-13:9781506179537

DEDICATION

To all who dream, then try their damndest to make it a reality.

CONTENTS

INTRODUCTION 1

CHAPTER 1 MOTIVATION: The necessary intangible 3

    10 REASONS WHY SMART PEOPLE INVEST IN REAL ESTATE 5

    READY - FIRE - AIM 7

    IN EVERY DEFEAT LIES THE SEED OF AN EVEN GREATER VICTORY 10

CHAPTER II RENTAL NICHES: The foundation of profitability 13

    THE MOST IMPORTANT THING IN REAL ESTATE 15

    HIDING IN PLAIN SIGHT 18

    NICHE NUMBERS THAT DEFINE SUCCESS OR FAILURE 21

    THE HEART THAT PUMPS MONEY 25

CHAPTER III NUMBERS: These define your success or failure 31

    THE IMPOSSIBILITY OF POSITIVE CASH FLOW 33

    HOW I MADE $3 MILLION IN 7 YEARS 36

    I LOVE NUMBERS! 40

    EXPENSES 44

CHAPTER IV TENANT CHOICE AND MANAGEMENT: Simple and to the point 49

    THE SLOB ELIMINATION PROGRAM 51

    I FILE FOR POSSESSION! 55

    HOW TO CONDUCT A HOME VISIT 59

    KEEPING "3s" 62

    EPIPHANY! 65

    THE TEN BEST TENANT EXCUSES 68

CHAPTER V RUNNING THE BUSINESS: The thing nobody is good at 71

    TORTOISE HIRING 73

    HOW I FIRE 76

    WHY MOST LANDLORDS LOSE MONEY 79

CHAPTER VI MAINTENANCE AND REPAIR: Stop the bleeding 81

    HOUSE MAINTENANCE - HOW MUCH? 83

    THE ELIMINATORS 88

    26 VIOLATIONS 91

    INSPECT WHAT YOU EXPECT 94

CHAPTER VII REHABS: The magic wand 97

    DIARY OF A REHAB 99

    DIARY OF A REHAB II 109

INTRODUCTION

FOR THOSE WHO ALWAYS DREAMED OF RICHES!

You, Dear Reader, have probably finished 8 years of grade (notice the word grade) school, 4 years of high (notice the word high) school and perhaps some university of higher (notice the word higher) learning. But did they teach you, along this boring road of sitting, subordination and testing, how to earn a living? Or even mention the word *wealthy* or *rich*? Of course not; because they are not rich and don't know how to attain wealth.

In my first book, the #1 bestseller <u>Buy & Rent Foreclosures</u>, I outlined the path I used, and here in my new book <u>The 7 Essential Habits of Wealthy Real Estate Investors</u> I dig deeper into the general concepts, unearth the here-and-now specifics, and give step-by-step instructions on exactly what to do and, even more important, what not to do. These are gritty, no-nonsense essays from the real estate trenches of how I do it. I make the complicated simple and the difficult clear—but yes, **you** still have to do it.

Study the lessons in both of my books, read the chapters, read them again, outline them, and discuss them with your partner or buddy. Join local Diversified Real Estate Investor Groups (DIG) in your area or other real estate investing clubs, find brokers who themselves invest, start visiting houses (at least two a week) and make offers. Sign up for my free newsletter, buy my leases, contracts and forms at *www.therealestateprofessorbaby.com* and come to my upcoming 3-day seminars.

You, Dear Reader, need to learn! And I am The Real Estate Professor! I will be your teacher. I take great pleasure when a student learns and earns. My objective is your success.

I have had many mentors help me along my path. Let me help you.

I BELIEVE THAT YOU CAN DO IT!

Joe Neilson
The Real Estate Professor

CHAPTER I
MOTIVATION: *The necessary intangible*

10 REASONS WHY SMART PEOPLE INVEST IN REAL ESTATE

1. **Largest market in the United States**
   You live in it, work in it, school your kids in it, vacation in it, etc. Huge. Filled with opportunities that no 800 pound gorilla, Fortune 500 Company or other bully can corner and crush the little guy. Perfect for the small investor who is the local expert.

2. **Banks will make loans with real estate collateral**
   Ever try to get a loan for a small business startup? Don't bother. No. Unless it has real estate collateral. Banks, especially the small local variety, understand the local real estate market. They have loaned in it for decades. They loan on the Real Estate, not the person. This is an advantage for the novice or an investor with spotty credit or worse. Present a pro forma, sing a sweet song. Approved!

3. **Niche Rentals**
   The Ace of Spades in a small investor's deck as he finds disparities in the supply and demand balance and invests in them. The imbalances are there because the market is so large.

4. **Tenants pay your mortgage and expenses**
   Tenants not only pay your expenses but also pay off your loan to buy the property! And after the loan is paid off, they keep paying! What a deal! How sweet!

5. **Inflation is your friend**
   The Fed is no longer printing billions, but trillions. The U.S. economy is sitting on the bubble of all bubbles. Inflation has always been the weapon of choice for governments choked with their own debt. Inflation raises, like an incoming tide, all fixed assets. Think real estate. Your mortgage, however, must have a fixed amortization.

6. **Forced Saving**
   What is the largest part of an average estate? The house. How did the equity replace the original mortgage debt? Forced saving. Every monthly payment, the principal portion is

"saving". Time passes (I know) at a future date the principal is paid off, almost magically, Presto! Gone. Where did it go?

7. Depreciation cuts your tax bill

Depreciation is a gift from a well-lobbied, irrational federal government, which being who they are, isn't likely to be abolished. Figure that out.

8. Expenses/own business may eliminate your tax bill even with W-2 income

I don't make the rules; I just play the game with a knowledgeable CPA who also has invested in real estate. Suffice it to say April 15th can be the cause of rational exuberance.

9. Lower expenses -- Appeal tax assessments

Taxes are generally based on the "reasonable" real estate value of the property times a percentage (11.5%, 25%, 62.5%, 72% etc.) which equals an assessment ($92,500) times the assigned mills by the municipality which is the dollar amount times the hundreds or thousands equals the taxes due, be it (a) municipality, (b) school system, or (c) county. Hire an appraiser ($325 per property) and an attorney who specializes in appeals who charges 25% to 50% of first year savings or 60% to 75% if he has to go to court with you paying the filing fee. With the recent property value decline, this is a no-brainer.

10. Mortgage paid off, life is sweet

It will come to pass. Time moves on. The 20-year mortgage is suddenly 10 years, then 5, then OVER! And it is SWEET! Start young. Persist. It will happen.

READY - FIRE - AIM

Why do you think some people are very successful while others with approximately the same intelligence and education barely get by? Studies indicate that acting with determination on current market opportunities is at the core of wealth building.

> *We do not find you on the list of Makers Good.*
> *Explain the fact!*
> *Ah no, 'twas not the chance you lacked!*
> *As usual - you failed to act!*
> *(Herbert Kauffman)*

PART I - WHY NOT ME?

Arnie, aged 68, living on Social Security. "Thirty years ago I signed an agreement of sale on a 10-unit apartment building, all one room efficiencies, on 19th and Locust for $80,000. But I didn't go through with it. I won't bore you with the particulars - but it was my wife. Today it would have been paid for, gushing money and worth $500,000, maybe more."

> "Of all sad words of tongue or pen, the saddest are these 'It might have been.'" (John Greenleaf Whittier)

Bob, a teacher, earning $53,000, 5 years to retirement. "My father had 10 rental houses in the Philadelphia art museum area back when a house there sold for $17,000 to $20,000. Asked me to help out. I was too young, too busy, too important. Now they sell for somewhere north of $300,000. That's $3 million easy."

> "Opportunity knocks but once. Regret a thousand times." (Unknown)

Matt, insurance salesperson, earning $46,000. "In 2008, one year out of college, a good buddy and I decided to partner and invest in real estate. He kept procrastinating, couldn't make up his mind, so I went ahead. Now I have 6 houses netting over $2500 a month tax-free. I don't discuss real estate with or around my buddy. He gets very upset with himself."

"Regret for the things we did can be tempered by time; it is regret for the things we did not do that is inconsolable" (Sydney J. Harris)

PART II   FEAR OF FAILURE, FEAR OF THE UNKNOWN

"The first duty of man is that of subduing fear" (Thomas Carlyle)

Fear causes paralysis in the face of challenge. Courage is needed, not to overcome fear, but to acknowledge its presence, face it as you would any obstacle, determine the next rational step - then summon up the character to take that step!

The following section should be reassuring to those struggling to purchase their first investment property. Well-located properties that I, with hindsight, believe I should not have purchased, over the long run made money. I call these "mistakes that make money". Perhaps you won't hit a home run with your first purchase, but as years pass you will round the bases and score! Read on!

PART III   WELL LOCATED REAL ESTATE - YOUR MISTAKES MAKE MONEY

Years ago, I mistakenly purchased a large, very old, wooden 3-story summer-only guesthouse without heat in a town along the Jersey shore. Twenty-seven rooms and two apartments. In summer months it overflowed with college kids who worked in restaurants, bars, stores, or as lifeguards. But the neighbors, town council, cops, and firemen HATED IT! HATED IT! After 10 years of battle the town, using the state fire code, forced me to knock it down. Which (Presto!) gave me two saleable lots two blocks from the ocean. Cha-ching! $150,000 into the till.

"Sometimes the biggest risk is not taking one" (unknown)

In my book, <u>Buy & Rent Foreclosures</u> Chapter Two "My First Disaster" tells of my first rental house purchase, a definite "mistake". (I would not buy it today.) About 100 years old, 12' wide, horrible condition, a winding staircase so tight that furniture, dressers and beds had to come in through the' second and third floor windows. But with a rehab and a good school district, it has stayed rented and nets $5640 a year.

"A man who never made a mistake never made anything" (David Gemmell)

In Chapter Twenty, house ID #16, a "mistake" that shows an annual loss of $2388 (my only loss of 68 houses). I purchased it for $79,900 and it is currently worth $194,400. Other benefits are, the municipality approved an additional lot worth $50,000, my mortgage payment reduces the principal $150 a month, annual appreciation of 3.5% as it's in the county seat, plus depreciation write-offs. Would I do it again? No, because it doesn't cash flow. Will it be a good investment? Yes, a very good investment.

PART IV   READY - FIRE - AIM

"What ifs" don't pay bills or fund retirement. Ready - Fire - Aim is advantageous only in a few situations in life: one is buying well-located investment real estate. It may seem counterintuitive that I also urge you to do your homework and fill out my Pre-Offer Property Worksheet (*www.therealestateprofessorbaby.com/store*), which forces you to research and do the numbers. But then you've got to grit your teeth, close your eyes, and make offers!

READY - FIRE - AIM

"The man who insists on seeing with perfect clearness before he decides, never decides."
(Henri -Frederic Amiel)

Realize you will never have all the information - nor will all the data be positive - nor will you be 100% certain of the outcome. And if you are absolutely certain, you are also certain to be overlooking something.

READY - FIRE - AIM

"To get a hit - you've got to swing." (Unknown)

I have lost money in the stock market, multilevel marketing and a few of my small businesses, but in the long run, I have never lost money in real estate. Over time, well-located real estate produces profit. Property values eventually rise. Rents increase. Net profit grows. Depreciation and business expenses shield your real estate profit, possibly your W2 income. Finally the mortgage is paid off and you have an oil well gushing green! Well-located real estate is the best and safest long-term investment. Period. Nothing comes close.

READY - FIRE - AIM

"If you want to learn to swim, jump into the water." (Unknown)

A realtor showed me a large, deplorable house in an estate sale. No one wanted it. I didn't want it. But behind the house, almost hidden by vine and growth, were six equally deplorable garages without roofs. I did the numbers, held my nose and made a ridiculous offer. Today it nets over $1000 a month.

READY - FIRE - AIM

Pull the trigger. Make an offer. Then another. Another.

"Only those who dare, truly live." Ruth Friedman

IN EVERY DEFEAT LIES THE SEED OF AN EVEN GREATER VICTORY

"What about my test results?" I asked the counselor as my teenage son, seated next to me at a large wooden conference table, studied his results.

She caught my eye, shook her head and turned to Bobby. "You have up to a seven-second audio delay. You're still processing the first part of a sentence as the teacher finishes. No wonder you're lost in a lecture-style classroom. Must be like they're speaking a foreign language."

Bobby nodded. "Says here my impulsivity is in the 90th percentile. Goal orientation 99%."

"You need to keep your mouth and emotions in check. But on the positive side, you're very social and empathetic. Balances you. On the whole it's a positive result."

"So I'm a qualified ADD guy then," said Bobby grimly.

"Yes, but remember the drawbacks can be positives also. Two sides of the same coin. In soccer you score a lot of goals...right?"

"I guess."

"You get the ball and head straight to the goal."

"I pass too."

"Your dad says you scored 26 goals."

"Yeah."

"Bobby, ADD is a talent. It has been kept in our chain of evolutionary advancement because it allows us to get things done that others can't. Mass public education is a very recent invention, less than 100 years old, and in that setting ADD can be a liability, but in the real world it can be a distinct advantage. Remember that. It's a gift."

"Okay. I think I've got it," said Bobby.

The counselor, looking down, started rearranging her notes.

"Bobby," I said, "Wait for me in the car. Go over the report and we'll talk about it."

Bobby thanked the counselor and left.

"You have my results?" I asked.

"I didn't want to go over them in front of Bobby."

"That bad?"

"Everyone is different. You're in business for yourself?"

"Yes."

"Good place for you. Ever been fired?"

"Unusual circumstances."

"Always is. Bounced out of school? Off teams or clubs?"

I sat back, somewhat shocked. "So I have it too. Genetic, I guess."

"It's largely genetic, but Bobby's version is different than yours."

"What are the advantages you mentioned?" I asked.

"Very visual, like a deer grazing, always looking around, impulsive, ready to react. Not an asset in some environments. But you can make decisions, are optimistic, have high energy, and are task oriented. A mountain surrounded by valleys. It's an entrepreneurial advantage."

I walked out to the car and got in. Bobby was smiling, holding back a laugh.

"You too, Dad?"

"Me too."

"Remember, it's an advantage," Bobby laughed.

"I'll try."

In accounting, each asset is matched with a liability--the books must be balanced. The digital universe is made of an infinite number of pluses balanced by an infinite number of minuses. This is the way all life is. It's a fundamental law of nature. So too are the talents of hundreds of successful real estate investors I have met. Each has his unique assets (+) balanced by its liabilities (-).

Whatever liability (-) you have, there is another side which is a (+) positive. You may be thinking, "Well, I'm different"....and of course you are. But whatever liability you have, there is a corresponding asset. Always. Law of nature. Your liabilities--if properly managed--turn to assets.

1. *I don't have much education.* Education? Who cares? One investor with 160-plus houses stopped at the 8th grade.
2. *I'm kind of pessimistic.* Advantage. You will make fewer mistakes. Did you know most good lawyers are pessimists? Many businessmen are too.
3. *I'm fearful of losing everything.* Fear is a great motivator to avoid loss. Hating debt is an advantage if used within a balanced plan.
4. *I have a full-time job and don't have the time.* Definite advantage. Most real estate millionaires started with a full-time job. Good for cash flow, getting a mortgage and your credit score.
5. *I don't have any cash.* Refer you to the original (about 1958) real estate best seller by William Nickerson <u>How I Turned $1000 into a Million in Real Estate in My Spare Time</u>, or <u>Nothing Down: How to Buy Real Estate With Little or No Money Down</u> by Robert G. Allen. Re-read my chapter on 100% financing. Creative financing is a blessing to the cash poor.
6. *I have a poor credit score.* Solve it. Beat the credit score bullies. Contact Neal Yeagley at *www.edityourcredit.com* (877-820-4509). Tell him you were referred by Joe Neilson from Delco Property Investors (DPI).

I could go on--but no doubt you have the concept. Whatever hand you were dealt, your talents and liabilities comprise a unique advantage in real estate investing.

The only talent I do see across the spectrum in successful investors is persistence and a strong work ethic.

"It does not matter how many times you get knocked down, but how many times you get up." (Vince Lombardi)

P.S.: I do see many successful real estate investors with what seems to be their version of ADD. High energy, risk taking, optimistic. But some eventually crash and burn. Stay balanced. It's not easy to do so. I know.

Chapter II
RENTAL NICHES: The foundation of profitability

THE MOST IMPORTANT THING IN REAL ESTATE

ALL ELSE PALES IN COMPARISON!
GET THIS RIGHT AND MOST EVERYTHING ELSE WRONG - YOU MAKE MONEY!
GET THIS WRONG AND MOST EVERYTHING ELSE RIGHT - YOU LOSE MONEY!

NICHE RENTALS. Defined as when demand for your offering outstrips supply. Sound simple? So does "Be happy!" "Follow your bliss." "Marry someone you love." The concepts are simple but the execution is not. And the execution is why so many landlords lose money. You need to understand, into the marrow of your bones, that a Niche rental is **MORE DEMAND THAN SUPPLY!**

HOUSE bedroom/bath	# OF APPLICATIONS FILLED OUT	# OF COMPETITIVE HOUSES	CONCLUSION
3/1 bad neighborhood	3	25	No matter what else you do, you lose
3/1 good neighborhood	2	17	No matter what else you do, you lose
4/1.5 good school district	7	2	No matter what else you do, you win
5/2 students within walking distance to university	4	1	You win
2/1 apartments within 1 block of hospital, government	11	2	You win

This is a numbers game. More demand, more applications, less supply, less competition = higher rents, longer stays.

Niches are, as Warren Buffet says, a good business -- where an 800 lb. gorilla (Walmart, Home Depot, McDonalds) cannot come in and destroy the small investor. If you have a good Niche, it is likely to stay as such for a long time.

Let's go over the important features that rental houses offer.

1. Location
2. Condition
3. Row, twin, stand-alone
4. Square footage
5. 2 bedrooms, 3 bedrooms, 4 bedrooms, 5-6 bedrooms
6. 1 bath, 1.5 baths, 2 baths, etc.
7. Kitchen and baths
8. Flooring
9. Oil or gas
10. Yards

Number One is Location, as in LOCATION, LOCATION, LOCATION - Which includes school district, municipality, neighborhood and block, all of which are important to Niches. Certain locations may be central to the Niche, such as close to work or school; i.e., hospital, factory, military base, university or government; or close to transportation, interstate highway or airport; or in vacation rentals, close to the ocean or bay.

Location is part of Niche, not its entirety. Niche is predicated on the demand for a house with certain features. An alert investor recognizes that certain Niches have more demand than supply. Asking other investors about Niches that have imbalances in Supply and Demand generally draws a blank, open-mouthed "What do you mean?"

Niches are central to minimum turnover, quick re-rental, long tenant stays (5 years +), six-plus applications per vacancy, and therefore profitability. Only with many applications can you rigorously screen, ask probing questions, wait for the prospect with financial and rental stability, perform many home visits, and choose the best candidate. With two applications your choices are limited. High demand = applications. You keep processing them until you get a "keeper".

I recently listened to a CD of a knowledgeable long-term landlord being interviewed by a real estate "guru" legend on landlording and communication with "residents". It was a good refresher covering such things as:

1. Curb appeal
2. Add-on rental amenities for a monthly fee; i.e., color of paint, ceiling fans, alarm systems, etc.
3. Call tenants "residents"
4. Positive win-win communication

5. Lease-purchase options
6. Automatic bank account deduction on the 1st
7. Payment plans for the 1st and 15th for an additional 5%
8. Marketing houses with local businesses and churches

I could go on - but I agree with these points and try to incorporate many into my rental marketing. But without demand, without applications, there's nothing to screen. If you have one or two it's difficult to find a stable long-term tenant. After all the marketing, showing and screening it comes down to the supply and demand disequilibrium of your Niche. With a house with heavy demand and short supply, you can be selective. But if you are one of 25 three-bedroom houses advertised in a bad school district, you may have to rent to anyone who puts nonalcoholic breath on a mirror and can sign his "X" legibly. Standards, point systems, home visits are all good, but they don't manufacture good tenants.

Let's reverse the roles. The best tenants choose the best houses within their Niche. Wouldn't you?

THE MOST IMPORTANT THING IN REAL ESTATE is recognizing imbalances of supply and demand and exploiting them by buying and renovating into fulfillment of the Niche demands.

Because of the overwhelming size and diversity of the market, there are always markets that are ripe for exploiting. My Niches are as follows:

1. 4-5 bedroom, 2-bath houses in good school districts, 70% to Section 8 tenants
2. Student rentals, usually 6 bedrooms
3. Garages to car enthusiasts and contractors

Write out your Niches. If you are not sure what they are, place ads for the ones you are considering and judge the response from Craigslist, Facebook and the newspaper.

If you are in a Niche where the supply is high and demand low, you're paddling upstream against a never-ending current. You may have FAITH that your marketing brilliance will work; FAITH that your open houses will be well attended; HOPE that you will receive more than 6 applications to screen; HOPE that you will find a well-qualified "resident". But the odds are that you will wind up as a case for CHARITY.

THINK the Niche through. Test it. Buy a house and see if you are correct. Then if all signs are go, turn on the afterburners!

HIDING IN PLAIN SIGHT

Finding Your Profitable Niche Rentals

You're trying to find something---You looked throughout the entire house and your car, twice---and finally found it---on your desk, right square in front of you!

A friend couldn't find his cell phone-finally gave up-someone called him-the cell rang-in his hand!

Christopher Columbus was looking for a new trade route to India and discovered the New World.

Wilhelm Roentgen discovered a strange photographic effect while experimenting with electrical currents through glass cathode-ray tubes. He called it x-ray.

We humans have trouble seeing reality. We tend to interpret current stimuli within the context of our preconceived thoughts, much of which is controlled by our normative culture-what other people accept as truth.

KEEP YOUR EYES WIDE OPEN!

You would like to discover the Niche rentals in your area that have more demand than supply, then buy and rent them and, hopefully, over time become rich.

You may have those Niche rentals "Hiding in plain sight" somewhere right in front of you!

Let's take a look at how I "discovered" my three Niche rentals. Hint: They were waiting for me, like Easter eggs waiting for excited children.

1. **4-5 bedroom houses in good school districts:** from the start, I decided I only wanted houses in good school districts--where people wanted to live. Seemed like common sense to me. I started buying 3-bedroom, 1-bath rows or twins--but bought a real estate book and course the described the advantages of 4-5 bedroom houses. I tested the hypothesis on

Craigslist and was surprised by the positive results. I became a "bedroom" finder and powder room maker. Instead of getting $900-950 a month for a 3-bedroom, I average $1300 a month for 4-5 bedrooms. That $400 per month makes all the difference. Remember that: $400 a month.

Bottom line: Found a Niche through reading and a real estate course.

2. **Student Housing:** I live 10 minutes from a small but growing Catholic university. At an open house, I happened to meet, and then rented to students for more money than I usually receive. This piqued my interest and I started buying large dilapidated houses within 1.5 miles of the school, rehabbing for 6 bedrooms and 2 full baths, and renting for $2000 a month. I have a tough student lease and have been successful. The closer to the school the better. More bedrooms, more money.

Bottom line: A chance meeting and initial rental pointed to the Niche opportunity.

3. **Garages:** I met my electrician in front of my two side-by-side 10 x 20 single garages, of which I was using one. He asked me, "Is anyone renting the other side?" I told him no. "Want to rent it?" I told him sure. "How much?" We agreed on a price and I immediately started renting garages I currently owned and looking for garages as part of any future purchases. I now have 26.

Bottom line: Chance meeting rented one garage.

My three Niches were HIDING IN PLAIN SIGHT. Yours are also. Open your eyes. Find one? Then do the math! (The math = Pre-offer Property Worksheet, part of my forms available at *www.therealestateprofessorbaby.com*)

REMEMBER, MY NICHES ARE NOT YOUR NICHES!

When I ask audiences about their Niches, it seems folks don't quite see their current rentals as a Niche. You may be in a Niche and just not call it such. The following are profitable Niches my audience spoke about.

1) A West Philadelphia investor, a handyman/contractor who personally does the rehab, maintenance, and collects the monthly rent was doing well but wanted an easier route. I said, "You have a Niche. More will come after the mortgage is paid off."

FIND NICHE - REPEAT - REPEAT - REPEAT - REPEAT - REPEAT - REPEAT - REPEAT - REPEAT

2) Tale of two areas: An investor told of doing well in one area (West Philadelphia) and very poorly (sucking all his management time) in another (Kensington). I told him to sell his losers-regardless of price-and invest the proceeds in his profitable Niche. He was elated. Seemed as though I had given him permission.

If you need permission for an "eyes wide open" Niche discovery---I give it to you!

3) Rent by the room: One investor does students; another Social Security recipients in North Philly; another young professionals in South Philly. There are 100s of Niches. More demand than supply. How do you know? Test the market with Craigslist or another medium, right to your cell phone.

A GALAXY OF NICHES:

1. Students - The closer to the university, the better.
2. Studios, 1-bedroom, 2-bedroom in areas that lack supply.
3. Seniors - Studio, 1, 2 bedroom apartments for seniors or for working women (you cut the lawn, give other services).
4. Hospital personnel - Adjacent to the hospital, nurse, doctors, administrative.
5. Downtown metropolitan areas - Young professionals.
6. Adjacent to government.
7. Disabled - 1st floor, ramp, disabled, possibly with meals.
8. Adjacent to industry.
9. Executive rental, studio/1-bedroom apartments for the weekday executives; i.e., Washington, DC by the Capitol.
10. Military - Are you near a base? Good demand for 2-bedroom apartments.
11. Vacation rentals - Various websites set up for this, picture important, VRBO.com is the dominant site.
12. Bed and Breakfast.
13. Event rentals.
14. Fraternity/sorority/club student houses.

Finding a Niche is like putting your wet finger in an electrical socket...you know it right away!

Bottom line: More demand than supply.
              You may already be in a Niche.
              Find Niche - REPEAT - REPEAT.
              Keep your eyes wide open.

They are out there. HIDING IN PLAIN SIGHT!

NICHE NUMBERS THAT DEFINE SUCCESS OR FAILURE

RENT - PITI = GROSS MARGIN - EXPENSES = PROFIT

What is your Business Model? I take as a given that you currently rent within a Niche, or if a Newbie, have conceptualized such (hopefully in writing), and now I urge you to follow me into the brutal foreclosing caverns of its numbers.

A BUSINESS MODEL sounds like a lecture in a MBA program or a boring business textbook, but it is the very essence of what your investment is or what you hope it to be. After the verbiage comes the numbers or pro forma. The numbers must be honest. The numbers must make sense. The numbers must lead to a profit, and a substantial one, allowing for the always-hidden, always-surprising, and always-recurring expenses. The numbers will tell you if your business model has a reasonable chance of survival, never mind success. Many investors, when forced into this black-and-white world of numbers, become quite creative in inflating the rental income, or substantially cutting the expenses and, to some extent, the PITI. Follow Dorothy and The Professor as we traverse the yellow brick road of investing, with the carcasses of those who failed providing a motivational landscape. Pick up a pen, print out this newsletter, fill in the blanks, and don't flinch from this grade school accounting gauntlet.

1. What is/are your Niche(s)? Do the best you can in 25 words or less per Niche.
   _____
   _____
   _____

2. What is a realistic rental amount for your investment? _____

3. What would you expect to get on an appraisal (after rehab)?
   $_____

4. What would you expect the bank to give you on Loan to Value (LTV)?
   $_____ (Currently I receive 70%)

5. What is the factor for the interest rate amortization schedule? _____ (Currently I am getting 5.75% amortized over 20 years, which gives me a factor of $7.03 per thousand.)

6. Your principal and interest payment is therefore _____.
   (Factor x mortgage amount)
   Your taxes are _____ (Look up the annual tax and divide by 12.)
   Your insurance payment is _____ (I average about $45 a month per house)
   Therefore, your PITI is _____. (**P**rinciple, **I**nterest, **T**axes, **I**nsurance)

7. Rental amount - PITI = **Gross Margin**.

   Gross Margin is grossly mislabeled by some Gurus or marketing pieces as "free cash flow", which is exactly what it is ***not***. Gross Margin is the amount that **expenses** are deducted from. Expenses, which most of the time defines a profitable house or one soon to be foreclosed on, include items such as routine maintenance, major and minor replacements or repair, tenant turnover rehab, lost rent, improvements, sewer, administration, advertisement, professional fees, district court filings, permits, and miscellaneous. After digesting this onerous list, the next time a Guru or marketing email mention the words "free cash flow" grab your credit card and hold tight---because they want to swipe it!

   Your rental amount _____ - PITI _____ =
   GM _____

   My standard (not goal) Gross Margin, not to go below, is $400 per month. What's yours

8. **Expenses** - I have written previous newsletters concerning expenses and suggest you read them---no, I suggest you study them---then calculate your expenses monthly on a spreadsheet using the headings listed in #7 above. Their sum is your budget total per month. If you can't define your numbers, it's difficult to target their reduction. Although this newsletter is on Business Model numbers, because of the central and misunderstood role of expenses, I will go over expense categories for a house.

   Rules of thumb:

   - Routine maintenance (major and minor), replacement, and other physical expenses are based on the square footage of the house, house type (such as row, twin or stand-alone), condition and tenants.
   - Administration - You may do this yourself, but after acquiring a bunch, you may not.
   - Sewer, tenant turnover, lost rent, advertisement, professional fees, permits, district court, advertisement and miscellaneous are very real and recurring.
   - Average expenses for a house. Depends on condition, tenants, implementation of "The Eliminators", tenant turnover, and average tenant stay:

Row/twin house	Low average - $200/month
Row/twin house	Medium average - $250/month
Stand-alone house	Medium (up to 1750 sq. ft.) avg. - $300/month
Stand-alone house	Large (over 1750 sq. ft.) avg. - $350/month

The following are Business Model Numbers. What are yours?

A) Business Model: 3-bedroom row in a bad school district
Rent $750 - PITI $600 = Gross Margin $150 - Expenses $300 (lost rent, turnover) = ($150)

Goodbye!

B) Business Model: 4-bedroom stand-alone in a good school district
Rent $1300 - PITI $800 = Gross Margin $500 - Expenses $300 = $200 profit

Not bad!

C) Business Model: 3-bedroom twin in just okay school district
Rent $900 - PITI $650 = Gross Margin $250 - Expenses $250 = ($0)

Hope you have a real job!

D) Business Model: Student rental within ½ mile of university
House rent $1900, garage rent $250, total rent $2150 - PITI $1100 = Gross Margin $1050 - Expenses $350 = $700 Profit

Sweet!

E) Business Model: 2-bedroom row in good school district
Rent $700 - PITI $500 = Gross Margin $200 - Expenses $200 = $0

Not worth the effort!

9. Fill in the numbers for your Business Model:

Rent _____ - PITI _____ = Gross Margin _____ - Expenses _____ = Profit _____

My standard (not to go below) monthly profit is $200 per month.

How does it look? Did you fudge and use the low-end expenses to make it feasible? Expenses are heartless little beasts and don't care if you are broke, cupboards bare and you are borrowing from your parents or kids.

~~~~~~~~

I have over 80 real estate books, many real estate courses (most purchased on EBay) and have attended many seminars and monthly real estate investor meetings, but have yet to find a teacher, a book, a seminar, or a Guru who will not only explain what I have gone over, but then lead you through *your* version of the Business Model Numbers, and then put forward his business model numbers. Here are my average numbers.

My Business Model: 4-5 bedroom/2 bath homes in good school districts, student rentals near a local university, garages for contractors and car enthusiasts.

Rent $1360/month - PITI $779 = Gross Margin $581 - Expenses $250 = Profit $331

You are an investor. Investors *must* make money...or they follow Dante's journey into the levels of Hell!

THE HEART THAT PUMPS MONEY

Your heart pumps nutrient-rich, oxygen-filled blood, ad infinitum, to every cell in your body and then carries the wastes back to be cleansed, then does it again and again as you go about life without giving it a thought or a thank you.

With a deep intelligence, far beyond ours, and which we have only recently begun to understand and appreciate, a trillion miracles a second occur within as you work, as you sleep, as you play, as you make love---every moment you are alive---all without you doing ANYTHING---no thinking, no planning, no to-do lists. You're simply not consciously involved, as your heart keeps pumping to keep you alive, every hour, every day, year after year.

Wouldn't it be cool to have a second heart, outside your chest cavity of course, that pumps money into your bank account in the same manner as your heart pumps blood? Pumps that green stuff every day, every month, year after year, while you sleep, while on vacation, while you are sick, while you travel---24/7.

Impossible? Actually, the history of business is brimming with examples, and it is happening today as you read this and certainly will happen in the future, but only to those who tap the deep natural intelligence (The Big Invisible Hand) that organizes the system (Capitalism) and mechanism (Supply and Demand) that creates wealth. It is the secret that it not a secret. It has produced thousands of books, movies, plays and countless dreams while the gurus dance like demons around the eternal flame of hope. The secret stands as Mt. Everest, but few see it, understand it, or climb and conquer.

What is the secret that is not a secret?

Let me tell you a story of my first introduction to the secret.

Years ago I was attempting to learn the real estate business and what segment of the endless variations I should invest in. I had read dozens of real estate books, attended seminars, and walked through a seemingly endless array of houses, duplexes, apartment buildings, shore property, and commercial rentals. I was a confused novice. Like a teenage boy at his first dance, I kept falling in love with whomever I danced with, till the next.

One afternoon I visited apartment buildings and houses with a salesman-broker working in his family business. It was evening and we were alone at his office. Sy was wearing drab, ill-fitting, non-matching "How does his wife let him out the door" clothes, socks falling, teeth crooked, hair uncombed, but he knew real estate and explained in some detail how he acquired apartment buildings, houses and a few commercial properties.

"So Sy, what do you think a guy like me should buy?"

"Ya really don't know much do ya?" Sy said with his superior Sy-why-don't you-get-your-teeth-fixed smile.

"You're right. Keep changing my mind."

"Well, sit down over here by me and I'll tell ya what my father told me, and his father told him. Ya ready for truth?"

I sat and leaned in. Sy came forward, our eyes a foot apart. "Yer goy - nice goy - once I was like you - not goy but not knowing nothin' - where to start - anythin' really."

"OK."

"Ya ready?"

I nodded.

"Here it is. I hope yer ready."

"I'm ready."

"**Own what people really want**." Sy looked at me expectantly.

Not knowing what else to do, I repeated, "**Own what people really want**."

Sy's big smile bounced up and down. Was there an orthodontist in his family?

"That's it?" I stared at him, hoping for more.

"Don't get it, do ya? Too young. Too goy. Last time. Now listen up. **Own what people really want**."

"Kinda like the Japanese poetry stuff - Haiku."

"Still don't get it. Takes a brain. Hafta think how to explain it to ya." Sy's chair slowly tilted back as he stared at the ancient yellow tiles seemingly about to fall from the ceiling, then suddenly jolted forward. "Why do some companies do good for - like what? 50 years? - they sell things people really want."

"Like who?" I asked.

Sy rolled his eyes, looked away and shook his head, then back to me. "OK. First grade - naw, kindergarten. Tell me about McDonalds."

"What do you mean?"

"Tell me what McDonald's sells."

I think. Sy squirms. "Convenient fast food at a reasonable price," I say.

"Do Walmart."

"Cheap everything." That's where the clothes come from!

"So maybe they have something people really want? Ya think?"

"Yeah."

"Do real estate."

"Well -- I don't know -- it's everywhere. People have to live somewhere, work somewhere, shop somewhere -- it's endless I guess."

"You guess endless? Endless? Naw. Ya know what the Torah says? Why do I even ask? It says location, location, location. True even for goys."

"I've heard of that."

Sy smiled. "So where do you live again? Don't tell me. Nice goy area, safe, good schools, low crime, activities for the kids. Right?"

"Sort of."

"So buy where people really want to live, work and shop. Ya got that?"

"Got it."

"Congratulations. That's half. Other half is...ya ready now?"

"Ready."

"*Waiting list*."

"You said '*waiting list*?"

"You should write this down or something."

"What's with the waiting list?"

"Take my friend from third grade, Morey. He owns a three-bedroom rental house in a place people like us really want to live. So he's making out, right?"

"I guess so."

"Forgetit. No *waiting list*. Why? There's twenty-five other three-bedroom houses in this area for rent. Morey advertises; no calls. Morey lowers his rent. Dirtbags show up, Morey takes them. Soon Morey prays for an empty house."

"So it's location where **people really want to live**, coupled with limited supply. Or as you say, *waiting list*."

"Yer catching it."

"Now what if there's limited supply but a big developer puts 300 three-bedroom houses in?"

"Hold on. This is real estate, ya see land is limited. My God or even your God ain't making it anymore. So is some nutcase gonna build new houses or an apartment building and undercut your rent? Naw. Too expensive. Not gonna happen. High demand, limited supply forever. Even you should get it, right?"

"If a tenant moves you can get another."

"Better. They don't move. Where they gonna go? You have what people really want and others don't. That's the point."

"So turnover is low?"

"Maybe even ya know, ya lose money to get a new customer, right? Keepin' customers, ya make money. Simple. Got it?"

"Yeah. Got it."

"Our customers don't have to drive or walk into our store. They live in it, sleep in it, friends over. Who wants to move? Pain in the ass. Takes a major thing for people to move. Don't give 'em one! Own places people really want to live, with a waiting list. Do I have to spell it out more?"

"I got it."

"About time. Last thing. Ya know I said 'really'. I'll spell it for ya.
R-E-A-L-L-Y. Like *really* want. Not want. *Really* want. Big difference. Don't forget it."

"I won't."

Sy sat back, finished. He looked around at the deserted office. Keys hanging on boards nailed to a plastered wall. Green army surplus 1950 desks. "Been away a month. Israel.

Wedding for a week. Family things. Stayed a month. Got back and everything the same. Rents in. Made money." He looked despondent. "Maybe I'm not needed."

Sy got up, offered a weak hand and ushered me to the door. "Don't tell any goys. My father would....don't tell any."

I don't know where Sy is. Rich, I suppose. But Sy's supply-and-demand equilibrium that really favors what you rent is the heart that pumps money. Own places people really want, with a waiting list. Your rental offering, regardless of which Niche you are in, must be supply and demand rafts floating down the river, always, always with the current. Never paddle against the supply-and-demand current. You will tire and you will lose and you will learn the sad side of foreclosure.

That's the secret that's not a secret.

Chapter III
NUMBERS: These define your success or failure

THE IMPOSSIBILITY OF POSITIVE CASH FLOW

Negative cash flow is the bitch that don't quit. It's the crux of why investors fall into the red abyss then burn in a financial hell.

Is your monthly bottom line negative? Borrowing from Peter to pay Paul? Let's analyze why. Let's go back to the basics.

1. Niche Rentals - What business are you in? Is it a good business or a bad business? (A good business has more demand than supply; a bad business more supply than demand.) Who are your tenants? Research and choose a Niche in the marketplace that has more demand than supply. Simple, but it's not easy. Think you've got one? Test it on Craigslist straight to your cell. Strong supply will fill your ear and press your start button. A positive Niche, once discovered and consistently repeated is the foundation of profitability. Note: All my Niches were standing naked in plain sight when I "discovered" them. (They hit me over the head while I was sooo busy.) Look around-see the obvious that's never obvious.

2. Pre-Offer Property Worksheet - Before making an offer, fill out this form, which forces you to project Gross Margin and Net. The form helps you filter out properties that don't meet a GM of $400 a month. That's not $400 Net a month. $400 Gross Margin (GM). Don't "fall in love" with a property, "fall in love" with a GM of $400 a month.(My Pre-Offer Property Worksheet form, my leases, etc. may be purchased at www.therealestateprofessorbaby.com/store).

3. Gross Margin (GM) - Must be over $400 a month. (Yes, I know I'm repeating myself, and I'm not finished.) Must be! Using the Pre-Offer Property Worksheet, estimate the:

	Rent	1100
Minus	Principal & interest	(450)
Minus	Taxes	(200)
Minus	Insurance	(50)
= Gross Margin		400

My standard Gross Margin (not again!) - not to go below - is $400 a month. My goal is $600+++. Some of my houses have a Gross Margin of over $1000 a month. Note: My average rent is over $1300 a month. If your average rent is $900 a month, the $400 Gross Margin may be a problem. Work the numbers over and over again. The Pre-Offer Property Worksheet will become your friend-and protect you from failure.

Less than honest gurus call Gross Margin (GM) "free cash flow", which it is not. Like NOT NOT. GM is the sum that ALL expenses are taken out of---that doesn't mean just maintenance- ALL expenses means ALL.
Gross Margin Examples:

Rent	900	1100	1300	1500
(PITI)	(600)	(750)	(850)	(900)
GM	300	350	450	600
Make Offer	No	No/Close	Yes	Yes

If your Niche RENTAL cannot give you a GM of $400 a month, look for another one. When filling out the Pre-Offer form don't exaggerate the rents and reduce PITI to make the $400 GM possible. Research the numbers and project realistic rent and PITI. Might use Zillow, Trulia or Trend to research the projected rent.

If you clear the $400 GM hurdle, you are only halfway there.

The following list of expenses is what I use in my monthly profit-and-loss report:

1) **MAINTENANCE** -- use 14¢ per square foot per month for a well-maintained simple row or twin house; 16¢ or 18¢ or even 20¢ for a poorly maintained house or one needing updating. The more amenities such as central air, appliances, carpet, storm doors, etc. the higher the maintenance cost per square foot. See my ELIMINATORS - 46 items not included in my rental houses.

2) **TENANT TURNOVER** -- the labor and supplies to get it ready for the next tenant. I figure $2500-$3500 per, but it can be a lot more.

3) **LOST RENT** resulting from nonpayment, eviction or tenant turnover or a combo of all three! The stronger the Niche, quicker the re-rent, the less the lost rent.

4) **ADVERTISING/MARKETING** -Rental commissions (I use a commissioned rental agent), newspaper, birthday, anniversary and Christmas cards with Walmart gift card, anniversary gifts and celebrations.

5) **ADMINISTRATIVE SALARIES** and payroll taxes (more properties, more salaries)

6) **OFFICE SUPPLIES** including computers, copier, phones, printers, toner, paper, etc.

7) **TRAVEL** - gas - car/truck purchase and repair

8) **SEWER/TRASH** - I pay sewer/trash

9) **PROFESSIONAL FEES** - CPA - year-end tax; appraisals if you are appealing taxes; legal advice

10) **DISTRICT COURT FEES** I file early and often

11) **MISCELLANEOUS** All the other stuff.

Novice investors may diss my list of expenses as "I don't have these. I do all the work myself." Your time is money. As you start with one or two rental properties, I encourage you to do the work yourself, but as you add properties, you will be forced to delegate and your expenses will rise, but hopefully not your expenses per property. Experienced investors, having been down this expense road, may add additional items to my list.

A truism is that expenses are almost always more than you budgeted. I struggle with the discipline to stay within budget. Unexpected things happen. Constantly. That's why you need a GM of more than $400 per property.

Gross Margin and Monthly Net Examples:

Rent	900	1100	1300	1500
(PITI)	(600)	(750)	(850)	(900)
GM	300	350	450	600
(Expenses)	(230)	(250)	(275)	(300)
Net Monthly	70	100	175	300
Annual	840	1200	2100	3600
Make Offer	No	No/Close	Yes	Yes

Expense rules of thumb - I tried budgeting expenses as a percentage of rent, but that didn't work. As previously stated, my average rent is over $1300 per house per month.

Experiment with a fixed budget. Try my expense categories. Stay on top of all costs. Cut where possible. Inspect what you expect. Use home visits when screening prospective tenants to eliminate 3s.

Summary: If your GM is under $400 a month, you may be toast, unless you can drive down expenses by doing the work yourself. (I have purchased Reader's Digest Home Repair Manual and given it to novice handymen-it's a good resource.) Once you have your GM over $400, then constantly stay on top of expenses - spend one dollar at a time. Real estate is a simple business, but not an easy business. Real estate is an alluring glamour girl/boy who quickens the pulse, but the other side of the starlet is the bitch of cash flow. You control it or it will control you!

HOW I MADE $3 MILLION IN 7 YEARS

As my book Buy & Rent Foreclosures explains, in 2005 I needed monthly income and decided to invest in rental houses. I had no interest in building equity, nor did I perform any work in the ensuing years to that end. How then did I stumble on $3 million? The equity COMPOUNDED BY ITSELF over seven years as an unintended consequence of my buying, rehabbing and renting houses.

"Life is a snowball. The important thing is finding wet snow and a really long hill." Warren Buffett

Consider my "hill" the market demand for well-located 4-5 bedroom rental houses. The wet snow is real estate's gift of compounding appreciation, for the most part from inflation.

The following are the five steps I used to build monthly cash flow, which also compounded my equity into the $3 million: (1) *Buying low* - you immediately gain equity, (2) *Rehab with $2 in "forced appreciation"* for every $1 spent - gives you a big-time hit in equity, (3) *Inflation* fuels annual compounding on a hard asset like real estate, (4) *Monthly principal paid* from the mortgage payment increases your equity, (5) *Substantial net income* of an investment house increases its value and equity.

Let's take these one at a time.

1. Buying Low

    I buy foreclosed houses from banks (REO) that need a rehab. I make "ridiculous" offers and sometimes get ridiculous buys. Buying low gives me instant equity.

YOU MAKE YOUR MONEY WHEN YOU BUY

	Purchase Price	Appraisal	Equity	Rent -	PITI -	GM -	Expenses	= Mo. Net
A)	80,000	120,000	40,000	1250	800	450	212	238
B)	70,000	130,000	50,000	1250	720	530	212	318 (33% more #1)
C)	60,000	140,000	80,000	1250	640	610	212	398 (67% more #1)
D)	50,000	150,000	100,000	1250	560	690	212	478 (100% more #1)

One of the reasons #4 has higher equity than #1 is because it was purchased for $30,000 less. Another reason is its higher net income.

2. Rehabs with "forced appreciation"

   Well structured rehabs can give you $2 in "forced appreciation" for every $1 spent. The concept is to do those aspects of a rehab (kitchen, bath, refinished hardwood, etc.) that will return 200% in "forced appreciation". Caveat: I do not always reach the 2 to 1 ratio.

	A	B
Examples: Purchase price	$26,000	$30,000
Settlement (2)	4,000	3,000
Rehab	20,000	30,000
Total Cost	$50,000	$63,000
Appraisal	90,000	125,000
Mortgage	(50,000)	(65,000)
Equity	$40,000	$60,000

   Therefore:
   Rehab A $20,000 x 2 = $40,000 equity or "forced appreciation"
   Rehab B $30,000 x 2 = $60,000 equity or "forced appreciation"

3. INFLATION'S APPRECIATION of hard assets such as real estate is an extremely potent force that compounds its value year after year. Examples:

   A) My parents purchased a home on Long Island in 1949 for $7900. Today Zillow estimates its worth at $790,000 - 100 times its original value in 64 years.

   B) I purchase a New Jersey shore property in 1976 for $70,000. Today it's worth $1,000,000.

   Let's follow one, five and ten houses purchased for $120,000 and assume the historical appreciation of 3.5% per year will continue.

	1 House Inflation 3.5%	5 Houses Inflation 3.5%	10 Houses Inflation 3.5%
Year 1	$120,000	$600,000	$1,200,000
Year 2	$124,200	$621,000	$1,242,000
Year 3	$128,547	$642,735	$1,284,470
Year 4	$133,046	$665,231	$1,330,461
Year 5	$137,703	$688,514	$1,377,028
Year 6	$142,522	$712,612	$1,425,224
Year 7	$147,511	$737,553	$1,475,106
Year 8	$152,674	$763,368	$1,526,735
Year 9	$158,017	$790,085	$1,580,171
Year 10	$163,548	$817,738	$1,635,477
EQUITY GAIN	$ 45,548	$217,738	$ 435,477

4. Monthly Principal Paid - Your mortgage payment is principal and interest. The principal paid is immediate equity. For simplicity's sake I will assign $150 a month as principal paid or $1800 per year. I will also add $120 of equity per house each passing year because as a mortgage progresses you pay more principal and less interest.

YEAR	1 HOUSE	5 HOUSES	10 HOUSES
1	1800	9000	18,000
2	1920	9600	19,200
3	2040	10,200	20,400
4	2160	10,800	21,600
5	2280	11,400	22,800
6	2400	12,000	24,000
7	2520	12,600	24,200
8	2640	13,200	26,400
9	2760	13,800	27,600
10	2880	14,400	28,800
PRINCIPAL PAID IN	$23,400	$117,000	$234,000

It's "FORCED SAVINGS" - Really quite beautiful - all paid by the tenant.

5. Substantial net income increases value.

    A) House A nets $1000 annually
    B) House B nets $3000 annually
    C) House C nets $6000 annually
    D) House D nets $10,000 annually

Using any method (ROI, CAP rate, cash on cash %) of estimating an investment asset's value, the higher netting asset is worth more. Sometimes a lot more. As an investment vehicle, House "D" is worth ten times House "A".

I am an "Accidental Millionaire" as I did nothing to accrue the $3 million other than purchasing, rehabbing and renting houses for monthly cash flow. I will note, however, that I did not "flip" or sell them, since I wanted the monthly cash flow AND they will consistently compound with inflation in the future. Neither should you ever sell. If you need money, refinance, as it's tax free.

The bottom line of making millions: Own assets that compound in value year after year without you doing anything - or as little as possible. Make money while you sleep, vacation or watch your favorite team lose on TV.

I LOVE NUMBERS!

BASEBALL NUMBERS: "No question, Babe Ruth is the greatest hitter to ever live! Lifetime average .342, on base % .474, slugging % .690, 2213 RBIs. One home run every nine at bats! No steroids either!"

FANTASY FOOTBALL NUMBERS "Peyton Manning, the sure first ballot Hall of Fame quarterback has a quarterback rating of 106, completes 67% of his passes, 7.19 per yard, 32 touchdowns only 9 interceptions this season. What's not to like?"

MONEY NUMBERS: A computer salesperson who invests in real estate explains his finances. "In 2011 my W2 was $57,500, owned 3 rental properties worth $560,000 with a $73,000 loss carry forward from the rehab so I got back $9623 in federal tax, equity was $176,000. In 2012 the W2 was $62,000, $10,200 federal tax returned, now 5 properties worth $920,000 and equity of $296,000.

HEALTH NUMBERS: A patient visiting a doctor for the first time. "I'm 5'10", weight 172, blood pressure 125/60, heart rate 71, cholesterol LDL 99, HDL 51, total cholesterol 174, glucose 107, triglycerides 96."

Numbers are the matrix through which we interpret and attempt to understand our world. They are tools to measure and then judge if our thinking and intuition is grounded. Numbers define your business past, present and forecast its future. Numbers are worldwide, are only meaningful relative to other numbers, and are fun--even exciting!

If you are not numbers-oriented - that's okay. Real estate's numbers are grade school simple. You can become acquainted and compile the necessary numbers by hand, by computer, or have a bookkeeper/accountant do it.

Remember, numbers are the signposts guiding you at midnight along an unmarked, unlighted, constantly changing journey. I urge you to use numbers, as Archimedes used his lever, to boost your power and fuel your profits.

*** NUMBERS TALKING IN REAL ESTATE***

The following is how I use numbers in my rental business. I'll give you the headings for some of my most-used Excel spreadsheets. The spreadsheets are updated in pencil by hand on our bulletin board as need be, then updated on the computer monthly. They have the date of the latest update on the bottom.

TENANT SPREADSHEET: The basics on the tenant. *Rating (1-2-3), Address, Tenant Section 8/cash, Phone #, Rent, Caseworker/phone #, Original lease date, Anniversary date, Municipality CO expiration*

RENTAL SPREADSHEET: Follows each tenant's monthly payment history. *Address/Tenant/Security Deposit, Rent Amount, Month, Rent paid, Date on envelope, Late and other fees* (for each month). (Date on envelope is date of payment.)

MORTGAGE SPREADSHEET: Basics on your mortgage. *Address, Mtg. Company, Acct. Number, Int/Years/LTV/OrigMtgAmt/Date, Current Amt Owed, P&I/Tax&Ins/Total Mtg Pmt, Taxes, Ins escrowed?, Mortg Holder*

BIG SPREADSHEET: The mother of all spreadsheets. Invaluable as a management tool. Most data is entered once and done. *# of Property (by date purchased), Address, Purchase price/date of settlement, closing costs, Improvements, Refi costs, Total cost, Appraised value, Assessment, Refi terms %/yr/LTV, Orig Mortgage Amount/Date, Mtg. Amount as of 1/1/xx, Capital Invested, Current value as of 1/1/xx, Equity as of 1/1/xx, Mort Pymt-Prin/Int per mo., Taxes/mo/Condo fee, Insurance/mo, PITI, Rent/mo, Gross margin, Adm/Mktg/Repair/Vacancy* (Expenses are 17% of gross), *Total Monthly Net, Annual Net, Cash on Cash %*

BANKERS SPREADSHEET: I cut out many columns of the Big Spreadsheet so I don't confuse the bankers and mortgage brokers. I give them just what they need, no more.

PROPERTY STATISTICS: Everything about the property down to the size of the HVAC filter. *Address, Yr. Built/Made of, Sch. Dist., Type/Stories, Lot/Roof, Int/Sq. Ft., Bed/Bath, Bsmt F/U/RecRoom, Sump or Fr. Drain, Clean out, Heat gas or oil/air or radiator, Filter, CA, Wtr. Htr. G/E, WD Hookup/where, Stove E/G, Other Appl, Trash Day, Garage Dimen, Deck/Shed, Frt Yard/Back Yard*

THREE IMPORTANT NUMBERS TO FOCUS ON

A) **OCCUPANCY RATE:** Mine is 95.6% in 2012. What's yours? Don't know? Let's figure it out.

Occupancy Rate: Total number of months available for rent of all your properties divided into the months you have substantial rental income. Months between tenants, while doing a Tenant Turnover Rehab, or vacant in various stages of disrepair or any other reason count as "available".

Example: 68 houses x 12 months = 816 months available for rent
Months of income = 780 months
780 ÷ 816 = 95.6%

95.6% is good. My goal for 2013 is 97%. For 2014 - 98%.

Note: I rent 4-5 bedroom HOUSES (mostly Section 8) in good school districts. I also do student rentals and garages. One and two bedroom apartments generally have a higher turnover and vacancy rate.

B) **VACANCY RATE:** The opposite of Occupancy Rate. My vacancy rate is 4.4%.
100 % - 95.6% Occupancy = 4.4% Vacancy Rate

C) **TENANT TURNOVER RATE:** The number of tenant turnovers, for any reason, divided by the number of units. A **vacancy** always starts with a Tenant Turnover. Generally, the more Tenant Turnover the higher the **Vacancy Rate**.

Example: I had 14 Tenant Turnovers (move outs under any circumstances) divided by 68 houses = 20.6%.

This statistic paints an important picture. 1 out of 5 of my tenants moved. Extrapolating this 20% means we have an average length of stay of 5 years. Our goal in 2013 is 10 Tenant Turnovers for a 14.7% rate, which would give us an average stay of 6.8 years.

By far, the number one expense a landlord faces is Tenant Turnover and the ensuing rehab and vacancy. The number one gross income (top line) reduction is vacancy. Therefore, tenant turnover is very important to your mere survival!

I suggest you follow the above three numbers on an annual basis, comparing year to year, as they will to a large extent define your profitability.

How do you minimize Tenant Turnover? It's not easy. It's many things. Let's go over them in order of importance.

1. **TENANT CHOICE**. The most important factor affecting Tenant Turnover is Tenant Choice. Do you rent to slobs, deadbeats and hoarders that you then must evict? Or unhappy, disagreeable, uncooperative people who move every full moon? We rate our current tenants 1 (excellent), 2 (good), 3 (poor) and by far those rated 3 cause most problems and are the movers. So don't let the 3s in. Sherlock Holmes the application. And visit their current home!
2. **HAVE SOMETHING PEOPLE REALLY WANT**. High demand and low supply to a defined (Niche) prospective tenant. With a waiting list. Our motto is "Dream houses for rent". Amenities such as nice kitchens and baths (2) with ceramic, spacious, and refinished hardwood floors.
3. **NICHE RENTAL** - More of #2. We rent amenity-rich 4-5 bedroom houses in good school districts mostly to Section 8 tenants. We also have student rentals and garages. Tenants don't move if they already have what they want and are well treated.
4. **GOOD SERVICE**. Emergency calls go to my cell phone and are responded to the same day. Normal Maintenance Requests receive prompt response time with a "Do it once...Forever" philosophy.
5. **PERSONAL ATTENTION**.
- When speaking with a tenant I ask about their family and their kids' activities. I compliment those who deserve it.
- Send birthday cards, anniversary cards with a graduated (longer with us/higher amount from $10-$50) Walmart gift card, Christmas card with a $10 Walmart card. All cards have a handwritten "Thank you for being such a great tenant" or "We hope you say in your home forever", are signed by a person, and generally mention something or ask a question personal to that tenant.

That's enough for now. My book, Buy & Rent Foreclosures (Amazon.com) includes more on this crucial subject.

CURRENT (14) AND PROJECTED TENANT TURNOVER (TT) NUMBERS - Vacancy starts with a TT. Cut TT and cut vacancy.

A) 14 Tenant Turnovers
    Tenant avg stay 5 years
    68 houses
    20.5% Tenant Turnovers

    14 Tenant Turnovers (20.5%)
    x $7500 (cost per turnover)
    $105,000 Total cost for 14 TT

B) 12 Tenant Turnovers
    Tenant avg stay 5.7 yrs
    68 houses
    17.5% Tenant Turnovers

    12 Tenant Turnovers (17.5%)
    x $7500 (cost per turnover)
    $90,000 Total cost for 12 TT
    (save $15,000 from 14 TT)

C) 10 Tenant Turnovers
    Tenant avg stay 6.8 yrs
    68 houses
    14.7% Tenant Turnovers

    10 Tenant Turnovers (14.7%)
    x $7500 (cost per turnover)
    $75,000 Total cost for 10 TT
    (save $30,000 from 14 TT)

D) 8 Tenant Turnovers
    Tenant avg stay 8.5 yrs
    68 houses
    11.7% Tenant Turnovers

    8 Tenant Turnovers (11.7%)
    x $7500 (cost per turnover)
    $60,000 Total cost for 8 TT
    (save $45,000 from 14 TT)

OCCUPANCY/VACANCY NUMBERS

What does a 1% or 2% increase in occupancy rate give your bottom line? My current occupancy rate of 95.6% gives a Vacancy rate of 4.4%

A) 4.4% Vacancy

83,000 gross mo rental income
x 12 months
996,000
x 4.4% vacancy
43,824 money not collected

B) 3.4% Vacancy

83,000
x 12 months
996,000
x 3.4%
33,864
Save 9,960

C) 2.4% Vacancy

83,000
x 12 months
996,000
x 2.4%
23,904
Save 19,920

Numbers: Use them. They are your unpaid assistants!

EXPENSES

The Cemetery of Real Estate Investors

Kids have nightmares they can't control. Parents have kids they can't control. Some investors have expenses they can't control...or won't even acknowledge the problem...thus, rental real estate becomes not the fulfillment of a dream, but the Nightmare on Elm Street. How about you? Expenses making you crazy? EXPENSES drive many investors out of real estate, some to financial ruin.

I have found no other subject in rental house investing that is so invisible, that is not written or taught, than expenses. I have researched the most popular real estate investing newsletters - nothing. Websites - nothing. The bestselling books - nothing. The guru/experts speaking agendas - nothing. Yes, it may be mentioned in passing, "control expenses", "cut expenses", but no numbers, no ratios, no strategies such as my almost-famous *The Eliminators*.

Why? Perhaps it's better to push the Nightmare into the corner, hide it in the unconscious. Better not bring to light the ugly and noxious truth even as it bulldozes your hopes to a pile of moaning rubble on a foreclosed empty lot.

In direct contrast, public companies' quarterly and annual reports are filled with expense totals, percentages against budget, and gross margins. These numbers are openly reported and enthusiastically followed by investors and Wall Street. Ignoring expenses is not the norm in business; it is the exception. And it is deadly and dumb.

I actively manage 70 houses and 26 garages. I deal daily with the nonstop tide of expenses. I study (not look at) my profit-and-loss monthly statement against budget, and consistently attempt to monitor and make adjustments to overruns. I don't do this naturally or particularly well---I force myself to do it.

For instance, I have a 3' x 4' poster board on my office door (It forces me to look at the monthly expense numbers several times a day!) with monthly totals for Rent - PITI = Gross Margin - Expenses (9 categories) = Net for each month and quarter, totals vs. budget.

If an investor is not calculating and monitoring the monthly numbers, he is not an investor; he is a speculator/mystic who leaves the making of profit to chance. Do you hope and pray for profit from the tooth fairy so you can gamble another day?

I have asked individual investors if they have a budget and track expenses. "I'm too busy." "I don't know how." "What do you mean?" "My CPA does it at year end." Don't you be one of the former.

HOW YOU CAN EASILY TRACK THE MONTHLY NUMBERS

Budgeting and computing monthly numbers is not complicated. Here's how I do it.

1. QuickBooks - As you write a check using the computer, QuickBooks allows you to assign it to a category and a house number. If you write checks by hand, perhaps in the field, I write the house number and category in the left-hand memo space and my part-time bookkeeper assigns it when it comes up in our internet "online" bank account as it is cashed. Therefore, all checks are automatically assigned a house number and category.

2. Expenses on Excel - For budget purposes, put the monthly numbers in the following columns across the top:

Budget/Jan/Feb/Mar/1stQ/Differencetobudget (DTB)/Apr/May/June/2ndQ/DTB/ etc.

I also have these columns across the top:

Collected Rent-PITI=Gross Margin-Expenses=Net

The expenses go down the left-hand column:

Repair/maintenance
Tenant Turnover Rehab
Sewer/trash
Administration/office
District court filing
Advertising/Marketing
Permit/License
Professional fees
Miscellaneous
Total

3. Write checks or use credit/debit cards, not cash, for all expenses. Write on check the house number and category; i.e., 212 Electrical, 518 Sewer, 4123 Tenant Turnover Rehab, etc. When the credit/debit statement comes in, I write the house number and category next to the expense and the bookkeeper puts this in QuickBooks.

4. Rent - I don't take cash unless there are exceptional circumstances. Record all checks and money orders in QuickBooks.

5. PITI = Principal (P), Interest (I), Taxes (T), Insurance (I)
PI is a fixed monthly mortgage amount such as $528.
Taxes: $2400 year / 12 = $200 mo.
Insurance $600 year / 12 = $50 mo.
PITI = $778 a month

Rent $1300 - $778 PITI = $522 Gross Margin - Expenses = Monthly Net

6. Standards and Goals. Standards are bottom-line numbers not to go below. Goals are numbers to optimistically shoot for.

Category	Standard	Goal	Comment
Rent	What the market will bear		I will lower rent for the right tenant to fill a vacancy
PI Mortgage	Shop for rate		Prefer straight line, most are 20 years
Taxes	High taxes = low profit		Appeal taxes. I've had 95% success.
Insurance	Shop insurance		High deductible ($5000), add liability blanket. No LLC
Gross Margin (GM)	$400	$500/$600++	GM is not "free cash flow". It's what expenses are deducted from.
Net	$200	$400++	Expenses not spent go 100% to Net

7. Expenses, the categories: I rent houses, which means the tenant pays all utilities such as electric, gas/heat and water. They are responsible for the lawn, snow removal and pest control (after 10 days from start of lease).

The following numbers are my budget for my 62 houses and garages. I also manage 8 houses for my kids, but those expenses are not included.

Caveat: I do not always "make" my budget. But the budget numbers give me a standard to judge my performance. They are the rules in the game of Net.

A) Repair/maintenance	4500/73 per house	See "The Eliminators" in my book.
B) Tenant Turnover Rehab	4500/73 per house	Cost to "turnover" about 12 houses (about $4000 per turnover a house) a year. Does not include lost rent.
Total A + B	9000/146 per house	Total of A + B = $146 per house per month for an 1100 sq. ft. row.

C) Sewer/trash	1500/24 per house	Can't appeal. Tried to have tenants pay sewer, failed.
D) Administration/Office	2500/40 per house	PT manager, PT bookkeeper, PT rental agent, all W2 income (not 1099), plus office expenses
E) District court filing	300/5 per house	File on the 11th. Make tenant pay.
F) Advertising/Marketing	500/8 per house	Newspaper, Craigslist, website, Facebook, signs, gifts.
G) Permit/License	500/8 per house	Municipality's charge for inspection and Certificate of Occupancy (CO).
H) Professional fees	500/8 per house	CPA year-end taxes, attorney/appraiser tax appeals, attorney for advice.
I) Miscellaneous	1000/16 per house	Gas, car/truck repair, tools, misc.
TOTAL:	15,800/255 per house per month	

If you maintain and administer yourself, it may be less--but don't fool yourself--keep monthly numbers. Do sports teams keep score?

Monthly COLLECTED rent averages $81,000 ($1300 rent per month) divided into $15,800 = expenses equal to 19% of rents. I quoted 17% in my book, but 19% is more realistic. If your rent is lower, you will have a higher percentage of rents spent on expenses.

Let's go over the basics again:

Rent - PITI = Gross Margin (standard $400/mo) - Expenses ($255 per house per month, and I have The Eliminators) = Net (standard of $200 per house per month). You must have adequate Gross Margin to take Expenses from and leave you a Net over $200 a month.

Summary:

1. Track your expenses on a monthly basis. Compare to your budget or develop one. Have a simple system. Use QuickBooks.

2. Implement your version of *The Eliminators*, according to your Niche, to reduce repairs and turnover costs.

3. Administration and management - Do it yourself when you start. Have systems, forms, checklists. (Buy my forms at *www.therealestateprofessorbaby.com*).

4. Turnover and its ensuing rehab and lost rent is your biggest expense.

5. Appeal your taxes.

6. Rent to a Niche where demand outstrips supply.

7. Have standard gross margin of $400 a month or more, with a net of $200 a month or more.

8. Rate current tenants and prospective tenants 1 Excellent, 2 Good, 3 Poor. Never, ever rent to a 3. Do a home visit, then run a credit, eviction and criminal check.

9. Every dollar or $1000 dollars not spent goes directly to Net.

10. Run your business like a business. You are not a social worker.

11. File often and early. Keep the process moving until you are 100% paid. Do not "satisfy" the judgment because of an "agreement". Most won't be fulfilled.

Real estate is a simple business, but it's not an easy business. Work it hard and it will not be hard.

Chapter IV
TENANT CHOICE AND MANAGEMENT: Simple and to the point

THE SLOB ELIMINATION PROGRAM

You will lose a lot of money renting to Slobs. Not $2000 or $3000 but a minimum of $7000, possibly $12,000, maybe $15,000. I know, because I have felt five digits of pain more than once. Not saying how many; after all, I'm supposed to be an expert and in this essay I am that, but on Slobs and their elimination (Sign up for my Boot Camp "Slob Detection for Non-Slobs". For five never-forgotten days you'll live in a deserted Camden, NJ row house, no utilities, no change of clothes, no running water, eat without utensils. Learn from the very best - actual Slobs!) But first, before I digress further and attempt to sell you other even more valuable things that don't exist, I list below the cost of evicting Slobs:

1. Rent $1350/mo. – Slobs are also Deadbeats. 3 months to evict. $4050

2. 40-yard dumpster – Slobs are also Hoarders. Demo house filled with junk. $1000

3. Paint, repair extensive damage, poly hardwood (rugs if you still use a Beeper), pest control, doors, screens, smoke detectors, mini blinds, etc $5000

4. Two months advertising, showing & renting to, hopefully, non-Slobs $1000

5. Two months rent lost during above @ $1350/month $2700

                                                                                   TOTAL: $13,750

Think $13,750 is high? Study the individual numbers. Might be low. Unless you do the work yourself or hire illegal immigrants or stop paying the mortgage, or...but wait...there's more!

6. Mortgage, insurance, taxes $800/month x 5 months $4000

                                                                           NEW TOTAL: $17,750

Getting ridiculous, isn't it? And that's just one Slob. What if you have two or three? Your investment dreams are floating, with other things, in the backed up, overflowing commode.

Now you really want to know about my Boot Camp "Slob Detection for Non-Slobs". You're itching for the 800 number, credit card ready - But wait! There's still more!

7. Constable, moving company, storage of their junk for 30 days $4000
(in my state of Pennsylvania, during an eviction, law mandates
Landlord pays above)

NEW NEW TOTAL : $21,750

All veteran investors please clean up after any newbies who have lost it.

Slobs are downright dangerous to a landlord's SURVIVAL! Never mind profit; I'm talking SURVIVAL! And since Slobs don't know they're Slobs, won't admit they're Slobs, and mix undetected in our midst like the creatures in Night of the Living Dead, how the hell do you detect them when choosing a tenant?

Got your attention? Good. Now my very serious 10-point Slob Elimination Program.

1) No homeless, no social services prospects or projects, no living with Mom or sister.

If I can't do a home visit at their current address where they have lived for at least a year, they are eliminated. Water and people find their own level. A landlord NEEDS the upper 50% just to survive. The upper 75% will make money. I pray that I am ruthless (such a good word; sounds just like it means) enough to remain an ex-closet social worker.

2) Four-Page Application

Prospects fill out our application (no application fee) over the web or at our open house. We rate the application by effort, completeness, neatness, intelligence, manners, dress and deportment (over the web some are not applicable until we meet) by 1-Excellent, 2-Good, 3-Not acceptable. This procedure forces the rental agent to start qualifying. If you question the "Discrimination" liability, I plead guilty of discriminating against Slobs.

3) Home Visit

A. Within days of receiving an application rated a 1 or 2, we visit the prospect's current home on appointment. Walk into all rooms, basement, and rear yard, open the oven, smell for pets, and speak with the kids. Clean. We want clean. Clean clean. Kids' rooms can be disheveled. But clean. Clean makes money. Renting to Slobs is voluntarily swallowing poison.

B. Slob evidence at Home Visit - Red Flags

- If there's a pile of garbage on the curb outside the house.
- If there's a room with a locked door and no one has a key.

- If the basement door is locked, nailed, etc. Basements are where a Slob/Hoarder starts their work, then like mold, it spreads.
- If the kids are surly, loud, not friendly.
- If the house is full of cousins, neighbors, sisters, babies. Do we rent houses to families or flop houses to Slobs?
- If the house is a wreck because the landlord "doesn't fix anything", maybe he's broke from fixing their damage. People are responsible for their surroundings.
- We rate the Home Visit 1-2-3. We now have two numbers (application + home visit) on each prospective tenant.

4) Nice is nice, but clean is mandatory.

Slobs can be nice. Slobs appear to be normal. Slobs make up great excuses and wonderful stories exonerating them from all blame. Nice, personal appearance, excuses, and stories are optional. You rent a house. Houses don't need nice, personal appearance, excuses or stories. Houses need clean. Clean is mandatory.

5) Research their application like Sherlock Holmes.

Call current and previous landlords. The current landlord may want to get rid of them, so he may lie, or just not take or return your calls. The previous landlord is a better bet. Persist. It's important. Also, Slobs sometimes go from job to job, have evictions or eviction filings, have criminal records. Red flags.

The next five points relate to your current tenant Slobs, their discovery, tracking, correction or eviction.

6) 30-Day visit
Walk through the house (like a #3 Home Visit, but more relaxed; we are looking for Slob evidence) 30 days after move in. If we have made a mistake, it will show. If there are problems we take pictures with our phone then mail a Violation of the Lease with the pictures, give 3-5 days to correct the problems. Why "problems" in the plural? With Slobs it's always plural. We then re-inspect. If they haven't solved the problems we take more pictures, to prepare for #9. At this point they understand we are serious.

7) Bill them
When we find tenant-caused problems that we repair or replace (other than normal wear-and-tear) we bill the tenant according to prices they have already agreed to in the lease. Small or large, doesn't matter. Take smoke detectors. We use the $20 (our cost) lithium sealed battery smoke detectors by Kidde. If missing, they are billed $40. They don't pay? Bill them again. Still no? After a stern WARNING letter, I file in district court. ("Tenant Charges" Part IV Section B of my lease has a full 8 ½ x 11 page of prices for just about anything, which the tenant has signed and agreed to pay if damaged. You can buy my lease, forms, etc. at www.delcohomerental.com)

8) File in district court for possession and a monetary judgment for the damage
Let's review. We have found Slob problems, taken pictures, issued a Violation of the Lease, re-inspected and the violations persist. We must now file for possession and a monetary judgment in district court. We have 12 pristine color photos of the house before the tenant moved in, 4 to a page, on 3 sheets of 8 ½ x 11 photo paper. In contrast, we have pictures of

the problems/damage to show the judge. The tenant is mailed a copy of our filing, then receives the Notice from the court with an appearance date. This threat of eviction may coerce the Slob to adhere to the lease and solve the problems and pay what is owed. Sometimes not. If not, go to court and win a judgment; but most importantly possession. The Slob may then repent. If not, evict.

9) Tenant Ratings - Our current tenants are rated 1-2-3 (1-Excellent, 2-Good, 3-Not acceptable) on a rolling year-to-year judgment based on cleanliness, damage and problems. We watch the 3s closely. We stop in to casually inspect. Drive by looking for telltale signs. Our handyman contractors give us feedback on cleanliness, damage, crowds and pets. During annual municipal or Section 8 inspections, a DHR employee or I attend the inspection of the 3s, looking for problems.

10) Discipline and Will - The landlord has the lease, the law, the courts and pictures. The tenant has excuses and stories. But the landlord must also have the discipline to follow procedures, enforce the lease's standards, and the will to win. Without those, 1-9 don't matter.

The Slob Elimination Program is proactive. We try our best to eliminate the Slob before move in. But if you make a mistake, pounce before it gets out of hand. Remember - it's a matter of SURVIVAL!

I FILE FOR POSSESSION!

"What do you do if tenants don't pay?" I asked.

"I file for possession!" roared Scully, his fist smashing down on a disheveled wooden desk as big as a pool table. The old man slowly and uneasily stood. He was surprisingly tall, ruddy loose jowls and a shocking lion-like white mane, red suspenders over an immaculate white shirt with a colorful, almost psychedelic 1970s tie held by a diamond stickpin. He grabbed a black cane with an elegant ivory handle and tip, and stabbed the air in my direction. "It's my house! You don't pay, we file! You get it Sonny?"

"We go by the lease", interjected Florence serenely, seated two feet to Scully's right, a well-endowed skirt-above-knees I've-still-got-it 50ish.

"Who are you? What are you doing here?" shouted Scully, his hand adjusting his hearing aid.

"He's a friend of your son," Florence said.

"Richard, eh? So what's this about? You selling something?"

"I wanted to find out how you've been so successful."

"Successful, eh", Scully turned to Florence, then back to me, his blue eyes spitting fire, "Who says we're successful? Who?"

"By some standards," Florence said. "Maybe not our own, but by most."

"How did you start buying so many houses?" I asked.

Scully hesitated, absorbing the question. The fierceness receded, reluctantly giving way to an uncomfortable state of indecision. He sat down heavily and looked at Florence.

"Go ahead, Charlie, tell him," urged Florence.

Scully's eyes softened as he sank into the shadows of his enormous black leather throne. "I was young, selling houses for old-man McGraw. There was this vacant triplex-almost falling down-estate owned-no showings. So maybe I'll live in one, fix up the other two and rent them. I had no money, so I did a no-money-down, them holding the mortgage, me starting to pay after I got them fixed. Sold houses during the day, did the rehab at night and weekends. They rented before I finished."

"Still has the triplex. Go on Charlie."

Scully's voice went down several octaves, the words delivered in a dreamlike cadence. "So I did it again. And again. Always living in the houses while I fixed them. Got a reputation with estate attorneys, if they had a dog, no matter the condition, I'd take it. After awhile real estate agents started bringing me their garbage. Bad luck cases behind on their mortgage. Anyone who really wanted out."

Scully, now into telling his story, turned to me, "Old Man McGraw didn't like all this attention I'm getting, so he calls me in and fires me! Blam! Ten minutes to clean out my desk." Scully snaps his fingers, "Gone! I'm shocked. For days I don't leave the house--don't know what to do--finally I wake up-Screw 'em, I'm a broker--I start selling out of my house, doing lots of deals, then half...," Scully chuckled, "then half of McGraw's agents knock on my door!" Scully laughed childlike. "I buy used desks, phones, turn the bedrooms into offices, knock out the kitchen. We start kicking ass!"

"Keep going, Charlie." Florence, enjoying Charlie.

"McGraw's pissed, so he hires a big Philadelphia law firm and sues me! Tries to put me out of business! What type of crap is that? After three days the judge throws it out." Charlie sighs deeply, satisfied in victory. "After a few years I have some money so I start making cash offers, ten day settlements, no inspections or nothing. The banks' foreclosure attorneys start sending me lists of their problems. I put a price next to some, send it back. Close 2 or 3 a month. Then the Seventies hit-interest rates 15%-18%--hard to sell stuff-I'm offering cash. It snowballs."

"The Nineties, Charlie."

Scully nodded, "Early Nineties--a real estate depression-bad time-some landlords taking a beating--one with....How many, Dear?"

"Eighty-six houses."

"Went belly up. I knew the guy. Houses all in my areas, so I offered the bankruptcy judge cash for all of them, the whole lot." Scully looked at me, "Understand by that time I had an open line with the bank."

"Charlie's being modest. He was on the board. Now he's chairman." Florence patted Charlie's hand.

"Then 2008 hit and it's been-what can I say-raining foreclosures. We pick and choose. Only in our areas. Get our price."

"The discount, Charlie. Tell him about the discount."

Scully lit up like a lighthouse. "I'm cheap-flat out cheap-and proud of it-- so I get the Scully discount or you walk. You get that Sonny?"

"Tell him what it is, Charlie."

Scully, stern again, "Fifty percent of whatever you offer. Doesn't matter what. You offer me a house for $1, I counter 50 cents." Scully closed his eyes, enjoying yesterday's discounted triumphs, opened them and looked at me as if for the first time, his mood darkened like a storm moving across a bay.

"What are you, like an interviewer?" Scully started again with his hearing aid, "What do you want?"

"I'm a friend of your son," I shouted. "Said you had over 400 houses, all paid for."

"What's Richard blabbing around for? He should shut his mouth!"

"What more do you want to know?" asked Florence.

"How do you manage it all? Must be difficult."

"What's this difficult crap? We find a problem tenant - we file. They cause police problems - we file. Behind on rent - we file. Give us a hard time - we file. You got that Sonny? We got the hammer, not them! Costs us $120 but raises a red flag - we're serious - you straighten this out or you're out. Joanne has been going to court for us forever. The judges know her and our lease - if we lose we appeal - get our lawyer involved. We have a system. Nice houses, good service. Maybe that's why some are with us 30 years - refer their friends, even their kids. Ought to write this down, Sonny. "

"And collections?"

"They pay. No excuses! No stories!" shouted Scully, "If they can't pay one month how they going to pay two? They want to pay the 1st and $15^{th?}$ No, it never works. Never."

"So if they are late...."

"Look", Scully's cane again jabbing air, "We file! Gives the tenant a kick in the ass. Wakes them up. This is serious. In court we demand a judgment and possession. Always possession. If they want a payment schedule, we'll write it out, they sign, but we get possession on their fulfilling the agreement. None of this going back and starting over."

Florence stands up, goes behind Scully and puts her hands on his shoulders. "After we receive the judgment and possession order, as the law states, we wait till the 11th day and file with the constable. He posts his 10-day eviction on the door. The constables know us and cooperate."

"What if a tenant pays on time but is uncooperative or disrespectful-won't let workers in...?"

"We file!" erupts Scully, "I'm in control. They live in my house!" The cane driving home the point. "I should rent houses to tenants who abuse me or my people? We file! Let them abuse someone else!"

Scully rose, like a mountain rising, slowly straightened up, his cane now tapping the floor, bearing weight as he walked around his desk. "Your time is up, Sonny!"

"And the houses are paid for now?" I asked.

"You the IRS or something? Who is this guy? You get out!" He pointed his cane at the door.

"I think Mr. Scully is ending this interview," said Florence.

"If you learned one thing, Sonny--I file! Now scram!"

"Where is that first triplex?" I asked. "I might ride by."

Florence, now arm in arm with Charlie, "You're standing in it."

Old Charlie with 400 paid-for houses and Florence the Fiftyish Fox made a very good pair, indeed.

HOW TO CONDUCT A HOME VISIT

Part of our tenant selection process is the Home Visit - methodically going room by room through their current home, including basement, stove, refrigerator, rear yard. Yes, we are nosy, nosy.

A good tenant is an ally, a positive force, a pleasure to deal with. We rate prospects, as they go through the selection process, as a 1-Excellent, 2-Good, 3-Not acceptable (slob, hoarder, deadbeat, uncooperative, belligerent, etc.). With tenants rated 1 or 2, you make money. With a 3 you lose *why-did-I-ever-get-into-this-business* money.

I anoint you Sherlock Holmes, viewing everything as possible evidence of the existence - not of the Abominable Snowman - much worse - of the abominable tenant, or as we term "it", a 3.

A "3" knows what is acceptable to the prying eyes of a landlord-to-be, and therefore camouflages, hides, lies, and distorts reality as best she can. It's a game - and tag, you're Sherlock. If you lose, it will cost you between $7,000 and $20,000, although you might not believe those figures. In fact, I just listened to a CD by a national landlord guru expert, and he quoted the average national tenant turnover cost as between $800 and $1,500! Hello! This is earth! What real estate planet are you on? Hey Buddy, you ever add up the actual numbers? Such as rent owed + uncollected rent while vacant + PITI while evicting or vacant + major damage + minor damage + paint + carpet (ugh!) + advertising + labor to rent.....and what if it's an elongated tear-it-up-before-I-leave eviction!...I will stop here, but....do your numbers. Be ruthlessly honest! It's shocking! Makes you want to get out of landlording or....perhaps choose a "1"-or if necessary, settle for a "2".

Let's go through what the Home Visit is...

1. It is your unusual opportunity to see EXACTLY what your property will look like after 60 days of tenancy. You can delete the prospect's stories blaming others, excuses,

wonderfully valid reasons, and soap opera scripts as to why her house is a mess or disaster. What you see - your house in 60 days or less. Guaranteed.

2. Sherlock looks for the telltale signs of slobs, which are close cousins to hoarders, deadbeats, and nephews to the adversarial and uncooperative morons of the "I am unhappy so everyone else should be". For your own sanity and net, SEE AND ACKNOWLEDGE THE CLUES!

3. "Be ruthless and cruel in judgment". It's difficult for me, being a "closet social worker", to turn down people who desperately "want" the beautiful houses I offer. But as Darwin said in the last page of <u>Origin of the Species</u>, "Nature is ruthless and cruel." For your survival, so should you.

4. Regardless of the outcome of your visit, don't disclose your opinion to the prospect. If a turndown, mail a checked-off innocuous form letter. Keep it general.

Planning the "Home Visit"
Sherlock Holmes' "Clues to Profitability."

1. Set up an appointment. Some say, "Come over anytime." Some hesitate, "I'll call you." Some say no, giving a feeble excuse. Let them go.

2. Tell the prospective tenant, who has already agreed to an appointment, that you will confirm the appointment one hour before the appointed time. You call and no one answers. Don't go. If you go and no one answers, leave. One-third of our applicants do not allow a Home Visit. They have things they don't want us to see. One out of three! So be it.

3. Arrive early. Drive down the street and surrounding streets. If there is an alleyway in the rear, drive down and inspect the rear of the prospect's current house. Garbage bags piled up? Where did they come from? Trash all over the place? Furniture?

4. Front lawn - trash, furniture, "things" in the front yard, side yard, pets, dogs tied up, people hanging out?

5. House - View from the outside. Sheets hanging over the windows, storm door half off, main door a disaster? SHERLOCK SEES EVERYTHING! IT ALL MEANS SOMETHING!

6. Knock! They answer promptly? Sherlock is friendly, talkative. He asks questions. Are they well dressed? The smell? Adversarial? Friendly? Kids friendly? Talk with them. Open? Closed? Surly? Teenagers?

7. Clues! No furniture. Little food. Beds are mattresses on the floor. "3". Definite "3".

8. Neat, clean, orderly? Or piled with garbage bags "waiting to move"? Hoarders can't control themselves. Slobs on steroids.

9. **Kitchen - Open the stove and refrigerator. Roaches? Clean-clean? Bathrooms - mold?**

10. Bedrooms - kids' rooms - Messy is okay, but not a disaster.

11. Locked rooms - "Open up. The investors have a rule. I see all rooms."

12. Meanwhile you're talking, questioning. Are there extra people living here? Who are they? Introduce yourself. What's your name? Relationship?

13. Basement - Always inspect the basement. Always. The hiding place of junk, crap, garbage bags. What you see is what you'll get.

14. Rear yard - Pets? Junk? Stuff? Neat as a pin?

15. Have a Home Visit checklist (therealestateprofessorbaby.com) and fill it out in the car immediately after leaving the house. You already **KNOW** what they are. If they are a "3", have courage, write it up. Put "3" on the page.

What if it's close?

They have put their best foot forward. If it's close to a "3", it is a "3".

Homeless shelters, social agencies (except Section 8), living with mom or sister, just moving in with boyfriend/girlfriend - NO. Think stability.

Objective: Looking for a resident that will stay 5+ years! How many years on the job? House jumper? Tenant turnover is the Landlord killer!

Sherlock uncovers the clues to "3s" before they move in...so they never do!

Keeping "3s" from moving in is not just important; it's the difference between success and failure!

Bear the weight of another month of non-rent. Never let a "3" in. Never!

KEEPING "3s"

I say to myself, "Look, if I evict that darned slob the Turnover Rehab will be at least $6000, then 3 months or more of no rent $4500, total about $10,000 and could be $12,000."

Conscience: "But she's a **3**!

To Self: "Yes she's a slob and hoarder, but somewhat cooperative. And Section 8 pays $1400 of the $1500 rent."

Conscience: "But you have standards!"

To self: "True - but I also have to make money."

Conscience: "You're The Professor! How did that **3** ever get in?"

Excuses to Self: "Mistakes from 2010 and 2011 when I was buying, rehabbing and renting 10 to 14 houses a year while restocking our current turnovers. I got sloppy - sent an employee out on the Home Visit. Let in prospects from a homeless shelter or living with relatives where we couldn't do a Home Visit. I could go on, but I'll stop here."

Conscience: "So now you're playing tag between evicting and managing your **3s**?"

Self: "Right. Sometimes you can make money on **3s** but it takes effort and time."

Conscience: "Pain. Paid for with pain."

Self: "Yes. Pain."

Conscience: "Okay, you've made your Act of Contrition - now educate your readers with your soul bared."

My long-term readers know I rate my prospective and current tenants 1 - Excellent, 2 - Good, 3 - Poor.

Once I have determined a current tenant is a **3**, I then decide if I am going to "actively manage" to turn the tenant around or file for eviction, sometimes to put pressure on the tenant to modify the unwanted behavior. If it's "actively manage", I then mail a Violation of the Lease form on which I write out the deviant behavior and a standard of acceptable behavior below which I will file for eviction. I include a copy of "Highlights of the Lease", which is part of my rental lease (available at *www.therealestateprofessorbaby.com*) with the pertinent parts highlighted in yellow and pictures of the problems, if applicable. The mailing is my "line in the sand".

Sometimes filing for eviction followed by the court appearance, then the constable posting the 10-day notice to move, is enough to change the behavior and solve the problem, at least temporarily. Notice I didn't say just file for eviction. I follow through with the court appearance. Let the constable post. Hold their feet to the fire of eviction as I manage the problem and have them modify the offending behavior, perhaps sign an agreement. If they are hoarders or slobs, I help them clean the mess and take it away in a pickup truck. But tenant habits die hard, and the messes may reappear. This is the landlord work that I don't like, but I do it.

Caveat: The main reason I have a 1-year lease followed by month-to-month with a 60-day written notice is if a slob/hoarder/deadbeat/relatives-everywhere is protected by being in the middle of a lease, I find the judge reluctant to issue possession unless it's past-due rent.

Teaching point: I will point out again that I file in district court as a lever - change/pay/or go - my will versus your problem. The filing is a here-and-now wakeup call; the court appearance more of same; the constable posting - the tenant looks over the cliff and understands I am very serious; if **still no solution** (be it money or a change in behavior) then fill out the last step court eviction form and issue the check for the constable for the actual eviction. In Pennsylvania they have a Pay and Stay statute - they can pay up to the day of the eviction. And some have, one giving the last $3 of the $2400 owed in quarters.

Teaching point: If I know or suspect there have been police incident reports (If police are called to a house for any reason, the officers fill out a police incident report, or PIR) I immediately file a Right-to-Know form for all PIRs in the last 12 or 24 months. The officer reports what is happening at your house. Next best thing to a video. These are **very** helpful in determining if a tenant has to be evicted.

Let's go through the whys and rules of keeping **3s**:

1. **Screen carefully** - Including the Home Visit and credit/eviction/criminal check.
2. **Three-month Preventive Maintenance visit** - After the initial move-in. You are looking for evidence of slobs/hoarders. See damage? Take pictures. Garbage bags filled with clothes everywhere? Pictures. Garbage and flies? Pictures. The tenant sees you taking pictures - they know it's for court.
3. **Visit 3s** - Once you determine a tenant is a **3**, issue a Violation of the Lease, then visit every three or six months, depending on the severity. Ride by. Grass high? Pictures with Violation of the Lease. Snow not removed? Garbage put out in bags, not cans?

Mail pictures with Violation of the Lease, cc Section 8 caseworker with pictures, if applicable.
4. **Why pictures?** (A) Tenant knows you have the goods on them. Nudges them to change, if they are capable of such. (B) Judges believe pictures, maybe not what you say. (C) Section 8 believes pictures. They don't want problem tenants. They have a waiting list.
5. **File if you find a problem.** That's the big stick - the club - use it as an "I'm very serious" lever.

3s are generally combo packages. Slobs are generally hoarders, and some owe money. Their life is a daily negative reality show. They may get negative/adversarial when backed against the eviction. Have standards. Use the court.

Why keep *3s* if they are a constant problem?

1. Tenant Turnover Rehab and lost rent is the largest expense landlords face.
2. Some *3s* turn around; a few appreciate your effort to organize them out of sloppy habits.
3. *3s* generally land in my least desirable houses. If I evict, after I clean up their mess, repaint the walls, poly the floors, fix their damage, it may be 2/3/4 or more months before I re-rent. If there is hope, I try to keep *3s* - but within my standards.

Working with *3s* stories:

- One of my slob *3s* - Garbage in bags on curb, guarded by flies. I get a municipal violation notice. Bought her 4 garbage cans with wheels and lids that don't come off ($60 each), 4 boxes of 33 gallon 1.2mm (not .89mm) garbage bags to use in the garbage can I bought and placed in her kitchen, gave her 2 mice treatments and 3 roach treatments. She's still there.
- Why? $5400! Rent $1500 - PITI $800 = Gross Margin $700 - Expenses $250 = Net $450 or $5400 annual. If I evict, it will take 2+ years to break even!
- Here are the numbers: If she leaves, I'll have a tenant turnover rehab that will cost about $6000 Plus 3 or 4 months lost rent $6000 + $4500 = $10,500. Knocks out 24+ months of Net.
- If I do decide to evict, I attempt to start the process in March, out in May, Tenant Turnover Rehab, rent during June, July and August.
- Or I offer to pay her to move. If I evict in Pennsylvania, I've got to hold their furniture and stuff for 30 days.

I have more stories, but if you are an experienced landlord, so do you. Enough.

The real lesson is, don't let *3s* in. Once in, manage them hard, evict if necessary and move on, hopefully the wiser.

EPIPHANY!

"To arrive where we started and know the place for the first time." T.S. Elliott

Epiphanies are fun! They are the WOW you experience when confronted by a truth blazing LED-like across your mind, but they sit awkwardly on the quirky realization that it was always there...but its meaning hadn't impacted your perception. I have found you can have epiphanies on the same experiences numerous times--like falling in love with your wife--again.

Let's transition to real estate epiphanies.

You, dear reader, know that the number one impediment to profitability is Tenant Turnover. It's the Killer. The Goliath dominating the monthly P&L. Cut Tenant Turnover and your average tenant stay expands as if on steroids, Tenant Turnover rehabs are reduced, marketing and showings hit ebb tide, and this add-to-profitability list runs on like the start of the New York City Marathon!

So how do I (and you) reduce Tenant Turnovers? I recently analyzed my turnovers in 2013. Yes, I went through each Tenant Turnover on paper and thought through its circumstances, then explored for similarities and trends, then asked what I could do to avoid those turnovers in the future.

My Epiphany: We landlords are the keepers of our gate to heaven or hell and "by thinking we made it so." Therefore, Joe, take the responsibility to eliminate prospective tenants who will be evicted or move (eviction being the number two money losing turnover--beaten only by letting a damage-doing deadbeat stay!)

Let's mine my 2013 data for the gold!

1. Number of houses for year: 68.33

2. 13 moves, but 2 were internal, from one of my houses to another; something I discourage but will do for good tenants who otherwise will move. Therefore, 11 moves.

3. 68.33 divided by 11 = 6.2 years average tenant stay. This is considered good and an improvement from 2012, which was 5.75 years.
4. Occupancy rate 96.05%, vacancy 3.96%. Considered good and an improvement from 2012, which was 95%.

Now let's analyze the 11 moves:

- Five Section 8 moves, good tenants. To reduce good tenants' moving, in 2014 I've just implemented All Star Anniversary Celebration visits (Thank you Mr. Landlord cruise and Jeffrey Taylor), bringing gifts, balloons, etc. to the tenant's home. More on that in another newsletter.

- Four Section 8 evictions of tenants, all of whom were rated a 3. As you remember, I rate prospective and current tenants 1-Excellent, 2-Good, 3-Poor. I evicted the four not primarily because of money (although that may have been part of it) but because they were a hoarder/slob, damage, adversarial, police incident reports, fighting with neighbors, uncut grass, etc.

- Two cash tenants evicted. Again, both 3s, but these evictions are money centered.

Trend: All my evictions (4+2=6) are 3s. Epiphany! Joe, you MUST do a better job of eliminating 3s in your tenant choice process! Simple to say, but difficult to execute in the here and now of "Oh my god, this is the 3rd month without a tenant!" or "Well they are at least honest about past evictions and seem nice."

My tenant choice must have a better filter. Fortunately, I am able to be selective because I have 6-plus applications for each open house because I rent in Niches where demand outstrips supply. If you have properties where supply outstrips demand--your house is one of many--it is far more difficult, or near impossible, to be selective.

Where have my selection processes failed me?

1. Eliminate those who you can't do or who fail your Queen for a Day Home Visit. Some examples: Living with mom or relatives, in a shelter, moved out of a condemned house, emergency voucher because of some heart-wrenching drama, their landlord won't allow a visit (Right!). Travel to their home even if it's an inconvenient, time-consuming trip. If out of state, demand pictures, but everything else must be VERY GOOD. What you see in a home visit is what your house will look like after 60 days. No home visit, no approval!

2. Eliminate those who have an eviction filing. Yes, I know they will have a great "Wasn't my fault" story. One of my 2013 cash evictions had a great story corroborated by her "current"? landlord. She was evicted within six months. My average Tenant Turnover costs a total of...$8000. My bet is that yours does also.

3. Eliminate the adversarial, uncooperative, negative, demanding, don't follow your rules, instantly attempt to control the process prospective tenants. It won't get better; it will get worse.

4. Do a credit, eviction and criminal check and judge wisely. Do you personally have an eviction? A criminal record? I do not demand great credit from a Section 8 prospect, but evictions - no. Serious criminal record - no.

5. Be cautious of referrals from other landlords. Ask the "landlord" how much the rent is and the address. The current landlord may wish to get rid of a problem tenant or may be the "nice guy" who just can't give a negative referral. Call the last two landlords, employers, etc. Time consuming but worth saving $8000.

The Real Estate Professor is excited about screening better in 2014! No new 3s in my beautiful houses! I rate 11 of my current 70 tenants a 3. I hope to lower that in the oncoming years through training/management and attrition. Perhaps I can raise my average stay to over 7 years! Perhaps 97% occupancy! All money in the bank.

Now it's your turn, friend. Analyze your data. See a trend. What's the solution? Implement the solution. Make more money!

THE TEN BEST TENANT EXCUSES

While scrolling titles on Amazon I happened across <u>Rules for Radicals</u> by the famous (infamous?) Saul Alinsky, the text that spawned the popular reality show Tenant School that recently replaced *Jersey Girls*. Feeling like a sentry having intercepted the enemy's plan, I greedily read online (I refused to give Saul's estate money) the chapters *"Why it's not their house"*, *"The Legal Rights of Squatters"* and *"The 3 Year Eviction"*. Amazon's algorithms then served up Saul's follow-up bestseller, <u>The Ten Best Tenant Excuses</u>.

You may have heard of (or even used) these excuses before. I mean, everyone (except me and my readers) lies a little. But this list is like the Top 10 Hit Parade-landlords hear them all the time. They're like jingle advertisements on TV; much of the time you can complete the tenants' sentence after the first few words. I'll now share the wickedness of <u>The Ten Best Tenant Excuses</u>.

1. **Mail**: The indefatigable "The check is in the mail" lives on. With the post office in disarray, the lost-in-the-mail excuse becomes more viable. Can be used two or three times by the same tenant in the same month! Mailing an empty envelope is good, but without a stamp is better-or perhaps try the wrong P.O. box-- it will be returned-then you can mail the proof of a "not my fault". How's "I'll put a tracer on it!" A "tracer"? Why don't you call the FBI?
2. **Check or money order**: Don't sign it - leave out the amount - or who it's to - or the old reliable don't put it in the envelope. Bounced? The bank's fault, obviously. "Someone stole my checks!" Endless possibilities.
3. **Victim Unlimited**: "Feel sorry for me" or "Are you my Daddy?" This Hall of Fame "not my fault" career move has tentacles that invade all excuses. The central thrust is to move responsibility away from the tenant onto the landlord.

4. **You're last in a long line**: Car repair - groceries - back to school - kids' medication - electrical shutoff - birthday, Christmas and graduation presents. Roof over your head somehow sinks to the bottom of the list.
5. **Be incredulous!** "What? You haven't received it? Can you check again?" "Are you sure?" "Of course I mailed it! Are you calling me a liar?" "It isn't the 11th time! Only the...ehh...6th I think." "I'll visit my post office!" Or a beautifully executed jujitsu move of reversing guilt, "Did you lose it? Check with your bookkeeper! Isn't it possible this is your fault!"
6. **Lost a job**: With a difficult economy, it's plausible, so you are in a quandary, and bolstered with their "not my fault" logic the excuse expands into a plausible reason not to pay.
7. **Health**: Doctor visits are good, emergency room visits better, hospital visits the best-- really irrefutable, after a Shakespearean "near death experience" soliloquy. Can be the tenant or anyone in the family or extended family or on the block, or even a stranger. A can't-get-out-of-bed flu is good, but buttress it with a weak, halting, please-feel-sorry-for-me phone call. Note: The sickness of babies and kids is a sweet spot. What can you say? It's a close call between death and health, but health is inexhaustible and death, for the most part can (should) only be used once.
8. **Death**: People die every day, every hour! Not so much the tenants, but their family members (mothers are the best) and friends die more often, and astonishingly, die again at regular intervals. And what can you say? "Send me the death certificate"? I only confront when it's the third time for same person.
9. **Forgot**: "I'm very busy!" So busy not working-it's tough. Kids went back to school! Someone had a baby! Post office closed-- 1st was a Sunday-or a holiday-or my uncle's birthday.
10. **Out of town**: Funeral-vacation-visiting relatives-traveling-taking care of a sick mother, child or grandkid. Limited only by your creativity.

"There are more excuses than drops of water in all the oceans!" Ghandi

Chapter V
RUNNING THE BUSINESS: The thing nobody is good at.

TORTOISE HIRING

QuickBooks is down, you don't know who's paid rent or how much is in the bank 'cause your bookkeeper and plumber took a $99 Gamblers Special to Vegas to count cards. Your cell pulsates with four plumbing service calls while three other houses are without heat and your HVAC guy's truck is in the shop.

You try to meditate then go to the gym trying to stay calm and make rational decisions, but the incoming tsunami of calls, texts and emails magnifies the qualifications of the prospective replacements and you make really stupid hiring decisions. The snowball rolls and gathers size down the hill called survival!

Do something! You hire a bookkeeper, she runs out at noon for her AA meeting -- then "Yo Boss! Me and the kids goin' to Phoenix 'cause my husband left to live with his cousin in Alaska!" – next bookkeeper interrupts personal phone calls to shout, "QuickBooks sucks and what's this pay online thing?"

You know zilch about bookkeeping, plumbing and HVAC so your business backs up like an assembly line whose union threw tools into the machines over a grievance.

Let's put this hiring circus on slow motion and try to be semi-rational. The following are the core criteria that successful prospects have—be it an employee or contractor.

1. APPLICATION – Employee 2 pages, contractor 1 page. Did they fill it out completely? What's their attitude? Go over it with the prospect line by line. Ask questions. Copy driver's license. Does contractor have a truck or van? Take a look.
2. SUCCESSFUL WORK HISTORY in their area of expertise. The marketplace rewards competency with success. Success brings wonderful references. The future mirrors the past. Yes, successful candidates are paid more, but incompetency is more expensive.

3. STABILITY – You want long periods of employment, housing and relationships. Movers move, pulling an encyclopedia of personal problems written on pink slips and heartwarming not-my-fault novels. Want to go through the hiring process again? Embrace stability, especially when you feel like the Roadrunner on Adderall.

4. WORK REFERENCES – Verify the source. Ask name of company, address, number of years of employment. Have list of specific questions ready. Ask references to rate various criteria as Excellent, Good, Fair, Poor. Would you hire her again?

   CONTRACTOR REFERENCES – Pictures, website, visit a current or recently finished job. Verify references (could be a buddy?). Ask references lots of questions, get them talking. Is the job a $15,000 kitchen or a $70 paint a room?

5. CREDIT, EVICTION AND CRIMINAL CHECK – For employees and contractors, our application gives us permission. Amazing what you can learn. Have you been arrested? Evicted? Stinko credit? I thought so.

6. Total Testing (http://www.totaltesting.com/). Have administrative candidates take a Personality Profile ($20) plus Intelligence test ($20). Very accurate and a strong filter. Take a practice personality profile yourself—like looking in a mirror.

Think of the hiring process as a gauntlet and only the best make it through.
Here's an outline of my obstacle course.

	Administrative	Contractors
1) Original contact	Craigslist References	Craigslist, open house at job site, 1 every 30 minutes, references
2) Application	2 pages, work references, permission to pull credit/eviction/criminal. Rate 1-2-3.	1 page, work references, permission to pull credit/eviction/criminal. Rate 1-2-3.
3) Interviews – two	Both interviews with you and an associate, if possible. Dig deep with specific questions, share job descriptions. Rate 1-2-3	Both interviews with you and an associate. Dig deep. Listen to the answer as well as what is NOT SAID. What can't he do. Rate 1-2-3.
4) References. No references, no hire	Ask questions to ensure the ex-boss is real. Have 5+ specific questions written out. Ask them to rate different qualities Excellent, good, fair, poor. You rate 1-2-3	Much the same, but include type, size and pay for jobs. Pictures and website are good. Visit a current or recently finished job. You rate 1-2-3
5) Run credit, eviction and criminal check	Yes	Yes
6) Total Testing – Personality Profile plus Intelligence	Yes	No
7) Probation for 1st six months	Engagement letter spells out 6-month probation period with a fire-at-will. Written job description which he signs.	Sign a job-specific contract. Give Rehab Bible with multiple-choice test to be handed in before 1st check issued. No test, no check. Doesn't work out? Doesn't get next job.

One may view this hiring process as too long, too arduous and unnecessary. No. The whole process can be done in a few days. What *is* long and arduous is having the unpleasant task of firing a new hire and going through the entire @@#%X! process again! That's kick-myself-in-the-butt stupid.

Simply put, the Tortoise Hire has you invest time up front so you don't have to do it again. It's the same approach I use in my tenant choice that results in an average stay of 6.2 years. If I can duplicate 6.2 years with employees and contractors, I will have time to slow down the merry-go-round, take time off, have fun, write, and travel. Isn't that what's supposed to happen?

HOW I FIRE

Ever been fired? I have.

"Joe, the branch manager and I want to meet with you in his office now," announced the new sales manager on the first working day of the New Year.

Hoping they wouldn't take too much time congratulating me for being the number-one salesperson, I followed her into the black and white Staples office-in-a-box.

The branch manager, three months on the job and armed with no industry experience, was seated, head buried in the latest spreadsheet of declining sales, dressed in his always-the-same uniform, a gray three-piece suit. Rumors abounded and betting was rampant if it was the same suit or if he had a closetful. He looked up, painfully in charge, and said, like a method actor practicing, "We're firing you. You have ten minutes to clean out your desk."

In a dreamlike trance, I looked from face to face, searching for clues, waiting for them to start laughing. "Are you serious? Is this a joke?"

"You now have nine minutes and forty-five seconds," said the sales manager, looking down at her watch.

"What's this about? What's happening?"

"You don't come to sales meetings and your paperwork is crap. You're a terrible example for the new salespeople," he said.

She added, "No team spirit. All you want to do is sell."

Same-Suit continued, "You're not a fit with what we're building, so you're gone." He stood up quickly, put one hand down to the desk to regain his balance, "Get up. We'll walk you to your desk then out the door. All company material stays. All."

I walked to my desk in a slow-motion daze. Employees suddenly deaf, blind and dumb parted like the Red Sea. I methodically went through the desk, with both managers taking turns peeking over my shoulders like nosy birds. In five minutes, I was being led prisoner-like to the execution exit door.

Now I'm on the other side and am sensitive to the hurt that is done in a termination, but, as owner, I am yoked to the responsibility of ensuring that all parts of the business work well, so we can survive. If a tumor exists, it must be cut out quickly before it grows and engulfs its surroundings. The following is my roadmap for surgical firing.

Termination is an emotional demolition derby for both parties. To help solidify the decision in my own mind I ask myself a simple question, which forces me rate my employees and contractors into three categories:

> #1 or BENEFIT - What a gem! Competent; takes care of the business like it was their own; honest, even about their occasional error, little management time.
> #2 or GOOD - Talented but... needs an occasional sit-down or confrontation (correction), written job description and procedures, but on the whole does a good job - with guidance.
> #3 or BURDEN - Cavernous black hole sucking management time, drama king or queen, incompetent, needy, dumb as a stone, defensive, deflects feedback.

The question is simple, quick, and accurate: **IS JOHN Q. A BURDEN OR A BENEFIT?**

Immediately the mysterious Muses of Small Business Survival confer and pour forth their J.D. Power feedback in a clear why-didn't-I-see-that Las Vegas billboard. Like getting hit in the chest with wisdom. The results are either #1-Benefit - What a gem!, #2-Good - can work with, #3 BURDEN-A black hole sucking management time! If #3, the fire alarm goes off! Terminate! Terminate! This question helps motivate me to do what needs to be done with little fretting or ping-pong back-and-forth. Business is a competitive race and employees or contractors who are three-ton anchors must go.

BURDENS - YOU CAN'T AFFORD IT

Running a "Do it once...Forever" business with as few moving parts as possible means eliminating BURDENS, because BURDENS don't fade away by themselves. They are there - waiting - then like "Old Faithful", they spew forth another problem that requires management time, effort, and energy-all in finite supply.

BURDENS - MUST BE ELIMINATED

I have tried other methods to reach and implement a clear-cut Fire conclusion - job descriptions, annual reviews, one-on-one counseling, confrontation---all are helpful, but the BURDEN question has the mysterious power to push me across to action without a squishy soft U-turn. The core reason for the termination is the Burden's permanency, knowing that the BURDEN is never going away. One more chance, better management, or whatever has been tried and won't solve this-it's in the DNA.

For additional motivation (which I sometimes need) to pull the Fire trigger, I compare a BENEFIT (#1) employee or contractor to the laggard. Wouldn't it be a gift if all your employees and contractors were BENEFITS? All #1s! And why not? The employee and contractors are 100% under your control; so why not all BENEFITS? All #1s (#2s are acceptable) Yes I can do this! So can you!

SPECIFICS OF FIRING

EMPLOYEES - We have job descriptions and a six months probationary fire-at-will agreement signed by both parties. If problems arise, we start by writing a letter, being very specific as to the violations. Include examples of the problem and a reminder he or she is on probation, or if they have been employed for over six months, that this letter places them back on probation. If items are serious, state that further violations will necessitate termination. I sit with the employee, hand them the letter, give them time to read and digest. We discuss the situations noted in the letter. If the employee is defensive, full of excuses and "reasons", you know it's a dead-end. Sometimes there is a second "warning" letter to solidify the reasons for termination.

If violations continue, write up a termination letter noting their probationary status and violations. Hand it to them. "It hasn't worked out. This is your last day." If they plead, cry or verbally attack, never change your rational decision with irrational pressure. After termination, get them out the door immediately! Not dissimilar to the manner in which they terminated me. The letter helps you build a case to eliminate employee unemployment compensation claims. If, during this process, the employee resigns-fine.

CONTRACTORS - Once you have confirmed a BURDEN, if the job is small (handyman type), simply don't rehire that contractor after the current job is completed. If the contractor bothers you for more work with phone calls or emails, write him a letter (I find it more powerful than email) saying no work will be forthcoming. If you must FIRE a contractor during a job, read your contract (my forms and contracts are available at *www.therealestateprofessorbaby.com*) for a way out. Then arrive at quitting time with a letter of termination and last check (if appropriate), hand it to him and say, "This is your last day. Give me the keys (no keys-no check). Take your tools and leave." Stay on the job until he leaves. Trouble? Call 911. Change the locks that day. (We use Landlordlocks.com so we only have to change the cores.)

In conclusion: A quick and decisive termination is the most merciful for all concerned. Stasis or inertia causes entrepreneurs to continually manage employees or contractors who are a constant BURDEN. It takes courage and determination to FIRE the BURDEN.

The BURDEN or BENEFIT question forces me to adjust to the facts, forces me to accept the reality and pull the trigger.

May they all be BENEFITS. It's up to you!

P.S. Generally, you can tell if you made a hiring error within the first month. If so, immediately start the process and paper trail for ending the relationship.

WHY MOST LANDLORDS LOSE MONEY

Are you a landlord who loses money every or most months? That's not surprising since most landlords lose money. I'm not talking about a 1040 loss after depreciation, segmented depreciation and other mystery expenses. I'm talking losing cash money-real green-every month. You can only do that for so long, then checks bounce, credit cards maxed, landlords metamorphose overnight into slumlords (no money, no maintenance), foreclosure, then you are unceremoniously booted from your "Once in a Lifetime Opportunity!"

Why is it so maddeningly difficult to make money as a landlord? Because real estate is an enticing paradox-it offers a product-a house. Everyone "knows" a house--been in thousands of them--everyone "knows" a tenant-actually been one many times-you may have been "thinking about" investing for some time-doesn't seem that complicated. You then read the Holy Grail Real Estate book, or contract with a double smiley gushing with millions mentor, or attend an "Only six seats left" seminar with 246 CDs, 14 books, 6 booklets and a glow-in-the-dark "Money is Good" orange badge, the whole shebang is only $5995, but for you, only today, it's discounted to $1995-Hold it!-my manager just told me for the next 10 seconds it's just $995!--and-Presto! You are GOING TO GET RICH!

Toto and Dorothy pull the curtain back and reveal the Wizard Guru and the dark side of the paradox. The real work. Not the fluff-actually doing it! And, as in most things, it's not as easy as it might seem. The following are the basic precepts that I believe failed landlords do not follow.

1. **BUY WHERE PEOPLE WANT TO LIVE**. Tenants don't want a bad school district, unsafe streets and deteriorating neighborhoods. Location, location, location. Would you and your family want to live on the block?

2. **BUY OR REHAB INTO A NICHE RENTAL.** Know your tenant. Make the supply and demand equilibrium work for you, and you will be blessed with six applications for every vacancy.

3. **AMENITIES**. Depending on your niche, stand out. New kitchen and 2 baths. Space. Hardwood floors. Student rentals-within a mile of the university.

4. **MARKETING**. It's the internet, Stupid! CraigsList, Facebook, website with lots of beautiful pictures, open houses.

5. **TENANT CHOICE**. Six applications, remember? Better to have a vacancy than a slob, hoarder, deadbeat. The Home Visit. Sherlock Holmes the application. Adhere to your standards. Credit, eviction and criminal check. I go over applications and make well thought out decisions at a meeting with two experienced people with good judgment.

6. **TENANT MANAGEMENT**. If you don't enforce the rules, why should the tenant? Follow the lease. File in court on the 11th. Nice guys finish broke. (My 29-page lease *www.therealestateprofessorbaby.com/store*)

7. **RENT minus PITI = GROSS MARGIN**. Our standard (not to go below) gross margin is $400 a month. An investor cannot make a profit on less unless he does the maintenance himself (Are you capable? I'm not.) and all the management (I am, and I do). $400 is your margin of safety. You say $400 is impossible? Out of my current 69 houses, 11 are below $400 in Gross Margin. My all-inclusive Gross Margin average is $584.

8. **EXPENSES**. Expenses are more than you project, more than you budget, more than you can believe. Believe it! The "one-time" expense keeps changing clothes and showing up. Start with The Eliminators - 33% saved off the top. Then process, manage, and visit the service work before you pay. Be cheap--but not stupid cheap.

9. **TENANT TURNOVER**. Always the largest expense. $3000 to $11,000 per Tenant Turnover includes all repairs plus lost rent and PITI during the months of nonpayment and vacancy. Yeah, I know, you do it for $1500 to $2500. Sorry buddy, that's not a light, it's a train. Let's go over what this includes: (1) Cleanout-dumpster? (2) Major repair (3) Major replacement (stove, bath, etc.) (4) Minor repair-replacement-(miniblinds, screens, smoke alarms, etc.) (5) Paint (6) Flooring (Please tell me you don't have rugs) (7) Months of no rent (evictions are negative Grand Slams) (8) PITI during no rent/vacancy (9) Advertisement-open house (10) Tenant Turnover Rehab is an opportunity to implement The Eliminators; unfortunately, saving money costs money.

Still at $1000 to $2500? Buy a calculator that works.

10. **ADVICE AND EDUCATION** from those who are investing successfully ***TODAY***. Join and attend investor groups. Read books and newsletters. Write out your investment plan. Attend seminars or buy courses by investors who are currently investing in the niches you are or want to work in. Seminars to avoid: (1) Motivational! (2) 10 Ways to Make Money in Real Estate (3) Niches you dislike or wouldn't fit your talents (7) Gurus who won't reveal what they own or manage.

Consider these 10 rules carved on stone tablets and descended from Mount Sinai. Moses found the people worshiping golden calves. Follow the 10 rules and you will have golden calves to pass along to your kids.

Chapter VI
MAINTENANCE AND REPAIR: Stop the bleeding

HOUSE MAINTENANCE - HOW MUCH?

Nobody knows nuthin'

Would you agree that the average monthly or annual cost of house maintenance is central to an investor's profit? Yes, of course. Therefore, let's survey the available information on this most important subject.

Professional Management

"How much does an average row house, 1100 square feet, cost to maintain a month?" I asked a self-described expert of residential management at his booth during a Landlording exhibition.

He looked puzzled, then smiled, "We can replace a hot water heater for $650."

"But I'm asking for a monthly average for all maintenance for an 1100 square feet row house."

"Well....we're very inexpensive - have our own handymen - and each house is different."

"What about a general ballpark average?"

He frowned, then shook his head. "I'll ask around." He was soon back with a gray-haired guy in a stylish suit from 1920.

"I'm the owner. What was it that you wanted to know? No such thing as average maintenance. No, I've been doing this for forty years and there's nothing like that. Everything's different." He nodded. He smiled. He was missing two teeth.

Investor Newsletters

The various real estate newsletters I receive have no discussions, no articles, and project no numbers on the average cost of house maintenance.

Investor Websites

The various real estate investing websites have no discussion, no articles, and project no numbers on the average cost of house maintenance.

Real Estate Investor Books

My 80 real estate investing books have little discussion (just generalities; i.e., keep expenses low) but no projected numbers on the average cost of house maintenance.

Real Estate Gurus

The various real estate guru's I have listened to on CDs and during presentations, seminars, web seminars, and countless REIA's monthly meetings have never addressed the average cost of house maintenance. Very strange, since house maintenance is central to making money, central to surviving.

Google House Maintenance, Average Cost

On the website Houselogic.com, they quote Directors Credit Union and Lending Tree.com as saying the average cost is 1% to 3% of initial house price. For a $200,000 house, that's $2,000 to $6,000 - Much too broad to be helpful. And did they say initial house price? From what year? 1940? And a $200,000 house in southern California may be 900 square feet on a slab, but in Maine it's a 2500 square feet colonial with a basement. Earth to Experts! Hello!

Coldwell Banker's site has an article estimating annual home maintenance as 1.5% to 4% of initial cost. What's with this INITIAL cost concept? The "experts" must be reading each other's articles. Worthless.

About.com - "A popular rule of thumb says that one percent of the purchase (initial cost again!) price. Of course, this popular rule of thumb isn't totally valid." Eliminate "totally" and we have a starting point.

The average cost of house maintenance is not a matter of fuzzy rules of thumb and vague bracket guesses, but a matter of systems, condition, life expectancy and the dollar costs of repair and replacement.

To build a house of a certain type, square footage and location (1850 sq. ft. ranch in PA, or a 2450 sq. ft. colonial in VT) there is an industry-accepted cost per square foot, such as $100-$125 per sq. ft. This is accepted by all parties, even experts.

Houses are made of SYSTEMS. To maintain a house of a certain type, square footage and location there is a corresponding cost per square foot according to various factors such as the age and condition of the systems. These systems have a LIFE EXPECTANCY, like us Homo sapiens, which depends on a variety of factors. Make sense? Good. We'll now list some of a house's systems and their life expectancy taken from various websites.

1. Plumbing - suggest PEX, PVC
   Moen faucets/diverter/showerhead, etc.   50 years

2. Electrical wiring
   Panel, service   50 years+

3. Walls   25 years

4. Hardwood flooring   Lifetime

5. Roof   25 years

6. HVAC
   a) Gas furnace   25 years
   b) Gas boiler   50 years+
   c) AC   15 years

7. Kitchen   25 years

8. Bathrooms   30 years

9. Appliances   10 years

10. Ceramic   75 years+

11. Doors (6-panel)   20 years

12. Landscaping - trees, bushes

13. Gutters, downspouts   25 years

14. Formica countertop   15 years

15. Windows-vinyl   35 years

16. Basements   35 years
    Sump pump   12 years

17. Stairs   50 years

18. Lighting   25 years

19. Ceilings   35 years

20. Attic   75 years

These systems must be maintained, then eventually replaced - I replace as many systems as possible, especially the mechanical, during the initial rehab and finance the rehab within the mortgage, generally amortized over 20 years.

Currently in my area of Pennsylvania, one can build a house for about $110 per square foot. A row or a twin is less expensive to build than a standalone. If we take our 1100 sq. ft. row house x $110/sq. ft. = $121,000 + $30,000 profit = $151,000 sales price.

U.S. Census - Quotes $3,300 maintenance per year per house or $275 a month. At least it's a number. But how many square feet? Average house is, depending on what part of the country, city or rural, about 2000 square feet. Using 2000 square feet, dividing it into $3300 per year equals 1.65 per square foot per year or 0.14 cents a month.

Examples at 0.14 cents per square foot per month:

Sq. Ft.	Monthly	Yearly
1. 900	126	1512
2. 1100	154	1848
3. 1300	182	2184
4. 1500	210	2520
5. 1700	238	2856
6. 1900	266	3192
7. 2100	294	3528

Now for our rules of thumb, but with numbers:

Systems are in good condition:

Rule #1: Take square footage (1100) times the base rate of $1.65 = $1848 per year or $154 per month. $1.65 is a medium rate for a house with systems in good condition.

Systems are in old or fair condition:

Rule #2: Add 0.50 to the base rate of 1.65 for a total of $2.15 times 1100 sq. ft. equals $2365 per year or $197 per month.

Systems are in poor (end of life cycle) condition:

Rule #3: Depending on how poor a condition, add $1 or $1.50 to the base rate of $1.65 for a total of $2.65 to $3.15 depending on condition. The other alternative is doing a complete rehab.

Rule #4: Implement my almost-famous "The Eliminators" * to lower your annual maintenance costs. It has worked for me. (Observation: When I purchase a house, generally in poor condition from a bank, I do a complete rehab and thus many systems are new and I have "eliminated" items that cause a lot of maintenance. Then I finance the rehab within the mortgage, paying off the rehab over 20 years on a monthly basis. But I have a rehabbed beautiful home to rent!)

Rule #5: A row or twin house has less maintenance than a standalone. Take 0.25 off the base rate for a row or twin.

Rule #6: Tenants rated a #3 (we rate our current tenants a #1 -excellent, #2 -good, #3 - poor) increase maintenance by 100% or more. Tenants rated #1 stay longer and have substantially less maintenance.

Rule #7: Tenant Turnover Rehab (TTR) or the maintenance cost to re-rent a turnover, is INCLUDED in the average maintenance costs, although I track that separately on my P&L and Excel spreadsheet. During the TTR you have the opportunity to implement "The Eliminators".

Rule #8: The less Tenant Turnover, the less Tenant Turnover Rehab, and therefore your maintenance costs will be lower.

*See "The Eliminators" in my "The Rehab Bible", my 20-page booklet teaching how to perform rehabs and maintenance. Use "The Eliminators" as best you can within your Niche.

CONCLUSION

1. There is little information about how much it costs to maintain a house.
2. A house is composed of about 20 systems, all of which have a life expectancy.
3. Maintenance, like building a house, can be reduced to price per square footage. For a house in good condition, $1.65 per sq. ft. is a reasonable expectation. Fair condition $2.15, and poor condition $2.65 to $3.15, or consider a total rehab and refinance.
4. A row house will have less maintenance - take 0.25 off the standard
5. A bad tenant (#3) can easily destroy a house, costing $10,000+ to bring it back to an acceptable rental condition.

Don't procrastinate or avoid tracking the expenses on a spreadsheet or spreadsheet software such as Excel. You can't hit a target if you don't know what it is. If you want to stay in the real estate game, you must track and control expenses. It's not an option! JUST DO IT!

I hope this has been informative. It has been so for me as well.

THE ELIMINATORS

"If it's not there - you never have to fix it." Aristotle

Are you spending too much money, energy and time on routine maintenance and Tenant Turnover Rehabs? Like to pass more inspections? Simplify your business? Give your houses one more WOW! factor?

I don't want to appear overly enthusiastic concerning a mere list of household items called The Eliminators, since it may appear to some as mundane or even boring, but I get downright excited when I think of the money, time and hassles that The Eliminators have and will continue to save me.

Addition by Subtraction

When I first read of The Eliminators* it seemed counterintuitive that I could easily make a property more profitable and more attractive by simply eliminating frequently repaired or replaced items. It not only works, but has exceeded my expectations.

Inspections! Are municipal or Section 8 inspectors driving you crazy? I have had an inspector fail a house because a storm door needed repair, a rug was torn, a dishwasher malfunctioned, a toilet paper holder was broken off.....I'll stop here. With The Eliminators these things, and many more, will not be in the house and therefore **NEVER NEED REPAIR**.

You may be thinking, "That won't work with my tenants," or, "That's okay for Section 8 tenants, but would drive me out of business." Here's the good news! Whatever Niche you rent to, from Main Line mansions to North Philly what's-holding-it-up rows, the Eliminators can be adapted to give you substantial benefits. I, for instance, have niches of (1) 4-5 bedroom houses in good school districts, mostly (about 80%) Section 8 tenants; (2) student rentals; (3) garages (yes, it can be adapted to garages.) In my book Buy & Rent Foreclosures_ in Chapter 16, *Smart Rental Rehabs*, I introduce The Eliminators. Let's look at a few of the major items that are *eliminated* from the house:

1. **Carpet is out - Hardwood is "in".** Everyone loves it! If you rent older homes (pre-1950), under the carpet is hardwood. It doesn't matter what condition it is in because a specialist in "refinishing" will sand, repair and poly it. Prospective tenants go gaga! An amenity! A big Wow!

   On other floor areas not hardwood, put down ceramic and use a specialist. If you need to install new hardwood (Lumber Liquidators) and ceramic (Home Depot) it is more expense than carpet, but not much. But - Once and Done! During a Tenant Turnover you clean then poly the hardwood, just clean the ceramic. If you own the house for the next 30 years, the cost of flooring is over!

2. **Storm doors** - If a tenant wants a storm door they can put it on and maintain it.

3. **Dishwasher/microwave/garbage disposal**- Appliances break and are difficult and expensive to maintain. Get away from appliances! The stove is the only appliance we supply and maintain unless it's a student rental.

4. **Central air** - If your Niche demands it, fine. My tenants use window air conditioners. For my houses that already have central AC, the lease makes the tenant responsible for the maintenance.

5. **Regular ($5) battery-operated smoke detectors**- Many tenants don't replace batteries. A few years ago Kidde began selling a sealed lithium battery smoke detector, guaranteed for 10 years, for $20. I jumped on it. I now pass inspections and smoke detectors take up zero money, time, and the never-ending battery battles have ended.

6. **Oil furnaces/boilers** - Tenants don't want oil-too expensive. Tenants let oil run out-oil company wants money to "restart" the furnace, money to clean the furnace, money to repair/replace parts, etc. Natural gas or propane is clean, no maintenance and no service calls!

7. **Ceiling fans** - They break, flush-mounted lights don't.

8. **Drop ceilings**- Needs maintenance.

9. **Trees, bushes, shrubs**- Tenants don't maintain them.

10. **Gas stoves, gas hot water heaters**- Electric lasts longer, less maintenance.

11. **Tenant responsibility to pay** - (a) gas, (b) electric, (c) water, (d) pests after 10 days, (e) broken for any reason window glass/doors/screens, (f) sewer backups they cause, (g) any damage above normal "wear and tear".

12. **Tenant responsibility to maintain** - (a) lawn care, (b) snow removal, (c) smoke and carbon monoxide detectors, (d) kitchen fire extinguishers.

I'll stop here, but in my *Specifications of Material and Methods* (my 20-page Bible on how to rehab a house) I am now up to 46 Eliminators. I am hoping to keep going 'till I can rent nothing for $1500 a month. (Specifications, forms, leases at www.delcohomerental.com)

I guesstimate that The Eliminators have reduced my maintenance and Tenant Turnover costs with associated administrative time and hassles by more than 33%. That's huge!

Prospective tenants and their perception of The Eliminators

Tenants make "emotional" and "visual" decisions when renting a home. They "feel" the school district, block and neighborhood. "They "see" the house's space (big), new kitchen with ceramic, two bathrooms with ceramic, along with the gleaming ice skating rink hardwood and pure white walls and ceilings. The items that are not there (The Eliminators) are generally not part of their decision.

I love **The Eliminators**! You will too!

*Thank you Michael McLean and Nick Cipriano, the authors of The Section 8 Bible, who originated the concept of The Eliminators.

26 VIOLATIONS

"Tom, do you realize how many violations you and your two inspectors just handed me?"

"Don't keep track. We write what we see."

"Twenty-six. There are twenty-six so-called violations in a house that's in good condition, and you three guys have inspected it every year for the last eight years!"

"What's your point? Are you saying that these are not violations?"

"Most of these violations are your opinion of what you'd like the Code to be. Show me the line item in the International Residential Code 2012. It's not there. Tom, remember, you're a Code inspector, not an opinion maker."

Tom's face sputters like a frying pan, eyes glazed over like a bully in the schoolyard, his fingers jabbing air. "I expect these to be completed when I return. You can't rent the damn house until I issue a Certificate of Occupancy. Get that?" Tom turns and starts to the door.

"This is crap! You're holding me hostage because you want to run landlords out of Smithville. You don't even go by the damn Code. Do you even have a copy of the International Residential Code?"

Tom does a 180, lip quivering, "All my credentials," his voice changing octaves like a hinge on an old door, "are in my office. I take classes and go to seminars. Where are your credentials?"

"My credentials are my tenants who stay an average of six years. I house people, give them a roof over their head. You don't give a damn what's fair or what the Code is. You make your own code. You're a Code inspector, not an opinion inspector."

"Don't like it, don't fix 'em; but no C.O. for you, buddy boy. Get the drift? Don't like it, take me to #%@@ court."

"The district judge is in your pocket. He's part of this sham and why no investors will buy property here, because you won't let us make money."

Tom steadies himself, takes a breath, "I suggest you stop shoveling s**t out of the hole you're digging for yourself. When you're ready to be reinspected, call for an appointment." Tom's eyes are drilling holes. "But no C.O. until every last #%@@ one is done and inspected." Finger jabbing, "And if I see tenants in here, that's when I file in court along with all the other @%#! landlords who don't give a damn about our town. I live here; you don't. My game, my rules."

"You forget this is America, a republic of law and I'm an American citizen with rights. You're not above the law or the International Residential Code!"

Huffing and sputtering like a locomotive on the sidewalk, Tom exits. The three inspectors huddle, talking and nodding.

~~~~~~~

I recently did get 26 violations (see *below) in one well-maintained house but the above confrontation is from my fantasized "wouldn't it feel good to let them have it!" I attempt to control my emotions and follow Dale Carnegie's book How to Win Friends and Influence People.

Some municipalities have given their inspectors marching orders to make the town very difficult for landlords to make money---and that means **very** difficult. If they are consistently outlandish in the issuance of violations and they hoard the C.O., they hope to discourage new investors from buying and force current ones to sell to owner/occupants.

As word spreads, investors won't purchase properties in the municipality, and therefore, the buyers will be homeowners. I can see their point to a degree. After a municipality has 30 percent of its housing stock in rentals, it makes it difficult for the town to have a feeling of "this is home...I never want to leave".

THE LITTLE MAN COMPLEX

The little man has low self-esteem and searches for levers to bolster his existential search for status and power. Given a title and opportunity to express it, the little man inspector attempts to increase his power and status by withholding C.O.s until all is done according to his opinion....not the Code. The normative culture within such a municipality is a "We/They"; that is *US* the town versus *THEM* the landlords.

In one of the municipalities, the inspection "team" is a party of three, one for general, one electrical, and one plumbing/HVAC. They find/invent violations in a competitive joust and thus the aforementioned 26 violations.

How do I fight this?

I attempt to get "underneath" the inspectors, to show respect, to cooperate and compliment where appropriate. This works in some cases, but not all.

If a major item is brought up as a violation-clearly not in the code-I will point that out. If the inspector persists, I will go to my vehicle and bring in the International Residential Code 2012 to go over the code.

The code is the law. The code official is like a police officer who enforces the law set by the executive branch and decided by a judge. An inspector doesn't write code, nor is he a judge. He enforces the code as written. Nothing more.

*26 Violations - 1 House

1. 4" house numbers in front can't be on door.
2. Anti-tip device for stove.
3. Window sill in kitchen is rotted.
4. Hardwood floors done without permit and last step is too high.
5. Rear R bedroom door needs repair and pins.
6. Bathroom has tripping hazard and termination missing.
7. Replace broken tiles in dining room area and termination needed
8. Rear deck has unsafe railing and floor boards.
9. Missing rear patio door screen.
10. Rear bedroom needs finished flooring.
11. Rear siding needs repaired and finished properly.
12. Finish repairing wall in kitchen sink area.
13. Paint all unfinished wood or properly finish.

PLUMBING & HEATING:

1. Heater needs to be cleaned and serviced by a licensed HVAC contractor and provide paperwork to the borough.
2. Heater needs to have a fully ducted return air. Not to code. Cannot use return air from mechanical room. It must go to 1st floor. This has to be done to the 2009 IMC and permit is required.
3. Seal around pipes under kitchen sink and install escutcheons. This also needs to be done for bathroom sink on 2nd floor.
4. Heater flue pipe needs to be sealed around pipe where it meets masonry chimney.

ELECTRICAL:

1. Front egress light must work, no bulb.
2. Following outlets must be installed correctly: living room and basement next to dryer area.
3. Light cover in rear and for bathroom lights.
4. The following outlets have open grounds: living room and front bedroom.
5. Outlet in living room next to steps and in kitchen next to doorway have hot/neutral reverse.
6. Each room needs 2 outlets.
7. Repair GFCI near water heater.
8. Proper covers on all outlets and switches.
9. Remove extension cord near water heater.

INSPECT WHAT YOU EXPECT

Billy Talbert, aged 30, wearing jeans and a tired soccer T-shirt, opened the door to his friend's apartment and was shocked, mouth open speechless, by thirty voices yelling "Surprise!" then bursting into a spirited "Happy Birthday to You"!

In landlording, surprises arrive costumed in both the positive and negative, mostly the latter. Landlording reality is a Dali landscape where the expected is transformed to a head-scratching "What the hell?"

The blind man has a cane or a guide dog to avoid catastrophe. Landlords must be constantly vigilant in seeking clues for an approaching steamroller crushing budgets and the hope of profits.

I present to you, dear reader, the landlord's "inspection" in all of its disguises, to lay bare the light of truth and defend against damage, pain and negative cash flow.

A landlord without regular and timely "inspections" is moving toward temporary or permanent failure.

Inspections - with contractors, handymen, tenants, municipal or Section 8 inspections, and employees, be they in the form of scheduled appointments, unscheduled drop-ins, "management by walking around", drive-bys, pictures or checklists. Inspections are a time-consuming necessity for survival.

"Inspect what you expect"

THE REHAB: Minimum of once a week. Write up any deficiencies and work changes and leave with the contractor. (Go to my forms for sale at www.therealestateprofessorbaby.com/store.) Talk about the progress, or lack thereof, as it affects the next draw. Money gets their attention. Compliment if earned, but **always** straight talk on things wrong or falling behind schedule. It's not easy to be the *Bad Guy*, but it's mandatory. I refer you to the book, The One Minute Manager - excellent book for those, like me, with a confrontational-challenged personality.

The One Minute Manager in a nutshell: If you find issues needing correction, look the contractor in the face, tell him what is wrong and when it is to be corrected. If you feel uncomfortable, perhaps tense-good; what you are feeling is what the contractor (or employee or tenant) is feeling. He will not want to feel that way again. Always write up the deficiencies, hand or mail to contractor, to be covered in next week's visit. Nice guys finish last-and broke.

HANDYMEN: We email the Maintenance Request to the handyman, who receives it on his cell phone, or we mail it to those technologically challenged. I meet with handymen on Fridays, payday, to go over the work in detail. I inspect -- in person - at least one of his jobs in progress or completed. He shows me photos on his cell of the rest of the finished work. Photos have revolutionized inspections. No photos-no check. Without inspections, even of your most trusted contractor, control is slowly sliding from you to him. Always be aware of who is in control in dealing with your handymen, contractors, tenants, employees, and your kids (not your wife-we know she's in control). It's very dynamic, always moving.

THE PRE-INSPECTION CHECKLIST to be filled out by the handyman before a municipal or Section 8 inspection, or after a tenant turnover. The checklist forces uniformity and attention to detail. Any deficiencies found during the inspection that should have been fixed during the pre-inspection checklist are discussed and the handyman is confronted.

EMPLOYEES: All groups have expected standards of behavior, called the normative culture, most of these rules are unwritten. A job description or a set of procedures will help establish standards - then the boss must confront, correct, and praise where appropriate. Notes of praise or confrontation are helpful. Again I recommend The One Minute Manager.

TENANTS: The endless battle for control.
(1) The home visit is the cornerstone of our evaluation of a prospective tenant. We have a Home Visit form we fill out and rate the prospects a 1, 2 or 3. (Buy my forms at www.therealestateprofessorbaby.com/store)
(2) Within 60 days of moving in, we do a "Preventive Maintenance" inspection (with a form and rating) of new tenants.
(3) We "drive by" our houses when in the area, writing down and taking pictures of any violations, to be mailed to tenants.
(4) Municipality and Section 8 inspections - We do a pre-inspection checklist visit, as mentioned previously, and also, if possible, attend the actual inspection. The municipal inspections are easier since they tend to do them one after another-all in one day.
(5) We rate our current tenants 1-Excellent, 2-Good, 3-Poor. The 3s are on a short leash and are "inspected" regularly with violations noted and mailed. If a 3 decides to move, it's okay with us. We started rating our current tenants in January of 2014 and had 11 3s; at the end of this year we will have 4.

INSPECT WHAT YOU EXPECT. It's the landlord's responsibility to ensure his expectations (standards) are met or exceeded, and there's only one way to do that: See it. Or substitute a proxy such as photos or a checklist. But never give up the personal inspection. Never.

Chapter VII
REHABS: The magic wand

DIARY OF A REHAB

Penn Street came on the MLS in mid-2011 priced at $59,900 from a private seller. Vacant for years. 4 bedrooms, 1 bath, 1850 square feet, oil heat, enclosed side porch that could be converted to living space. Good school district. High taxes, but can be appealed.

Surrounded by large trees that need to be cut down. Three junk vehicles next to house. House needs a complete rehab including all mechanical systems.

Entrance driveway needs repaving. Negative - next to railroad trestle – hear trains go by and the engineer sings Johnny Cash

Family FHA buyers can't mortgage the house because of its condition. Investors are the only option, but the extent of the rehab scares some away. House is over 100 years old. Coal bin in small, wet basement.

Living room

Dining room

Kitchen

Side porch (bdrm, office, full bath)

1st floor bedroom (#1)

2nd floor bedroom (#2)

2nd floor bedroom (#3)

2nd floor bedroom (#4)

2nd floor bedroom (2 bedrooms (#5))

2nd floor bathroom

In 2011, with the lockbox number, I went through and visualized 6 to 7 bedrooms and 2 full bathrooms after rehab. I project rent from $1650 to $1750, possibly from Section 8. House in its deplorable condition is grossly overpriced and I'm busy rehabbing others, so I don't offer. A year later, in mid-2012, I visit again after they drop the price to $39,900 and offer $15,000 cash, no inspections, settle in 30 days. They counter at $25,000. I stay at $15,000. In March of 2013 I'm hungry for houses and revisit and again offer $15,000. Still at $39,000, they drop to $25,000 again. I counter at $17,000. They counter at $24,000. I give them my best and last at $20,000. The brokers kick in a portion of their commission and the seller accepts the $20,000 offered.

I estimate the rehab will (hopefully) be south of $70,000. I have the lockbox combination so I immediately start showing it to contractors to get bids before settlement.

We settle in the morning the first week of June and start the demo with the GC that afternoon. The electrician runs his wires, makes his holes, the plumber the same; GC fills two dumpsters and is working on the third. We take out the chimney all the way up to clear out a "new" bedroom. Don't need chimney since new gas furnace is over 92% efficient and we can PVC the exhaust out the side of the basement.

I meet with drywall companies from Craigslist to hang 300 sheets of 3/8, put on 3 coats of spackle, sand and prime. Prices are $10 to $30 per sheet. I settle on $14. Rip-off artists abound, so I'm careful. I settle on $14. Call referrals – no friends or relatives – I want real investors – ask how many sheets at what price – then the address – see if they are real. I settle on $14.

I accompany the GC, electrician and plumber to Home Depot and buy $6000 worth of material for $5000 in the "Bid Room". Have 7 days to add to the total with the same discount, which is figured by Home Depot's computer. I have all delivered.

Mid-July we pass the rough electrical and plumbing inspection. The drywall crew starts this week.

HERE WE ARE WITH REHAB 1/3 DONE:

Living room

Kitchen and dining room

Side porch   (bedroom, office, full bath)   1st floor bedroom (#1)

2nd floor bedroom (#2)   2nd floor bedroom (#3)

2nd floor bedroom (#4)   2nd floor bdrm (#5)(2 bdrms)   2nd floor bathroom

DRYWALL DECISIONS

We needed to install 320 sheets of 3/8 drywall throughout the property. That's way too many for a GC, so I needed a drywall company. In my location, a suburb of Philadelphia, drywall is done inexpensively "7/8 to hang; 7/8 to spackle twice and sand ready for paint".

I put an ad on Craigslist and on a Saturday scheduled the appointments every half hour. I have a one-page contractor "application" which includes all pertinent information including referrals. It was a close-call between a group from Philadelphia and Hispanics from across the river in New Jersey. I called the referrals for both and they were good; but unless you actually go out and see the work, you really don't know who you are talking to. In retrospect, the

Philadelphia contractor spoke English and was a pretty good salesman. He got the job. For a very short time.

I had the drywall and all other pertinent material on the site when they arrived late in an old beat-up Buick (no pick-up truck?). I alerted my GC who was working on the site to give me a report at the end of the day as to their progress, or lack thereof. He called me and said, "You've got to come over and see this."

The next morning I was on the site, and not only had the drywall contractor only done one room, but they had installed the sheets horizontally as opposed to the standard methodology of vertically. I immediately told him he was off the job. He didn't even argue with me, because he knew he was way over his head. I felt dumb, because I had made a dumb decision.

I immediately called the Hispanic contractor and through his wife, who spoke English, we agreed on a price and that they would start tomorrow. They were fast and they were good, and there was no more B.S.

Contractor lessons:
1. Hold your good contractors close to you.
2. Fire bad contractors.
3. Contractor turnover is, like tenant turnover, a fact of life.
4. I use referrals and Craigslist to troll for new contractors.

So, here we are, 2/3 finished:

Driveway

Living room

Kitchen and dining room

Side porch (office space, bedroom)

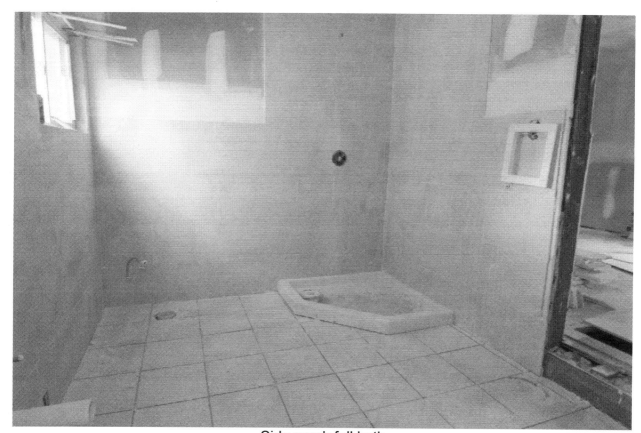
Side porch full bath

First floor bedroom (#1)

Second floor bedroom (#2)

Second floor bedroom (#3)

Second floor bedroom (#4)

Second floor bedroom (#5) (2 bedrooms)

THE REHAB IS FINISHED!

The house was rented for $1725 a month during the rehab. As with this house, we take before and after pictures of our rehabs.

The rehab was 80 days. Tenant moved in for a September 1st lease.

The parking lot is spacious.

Parking lot before and after

The floors came out well. A few of the pictures don't show the floors well, but they are beautiful.

Living room   Dining room   Kitchen

Notice how we used the covered porch to add a full bath and extra living space.

Side porch (full bathroom)   Side porch (bedroom, office)

Many times we use Home Depot's "Wall Closets". Cheap and quick!

1st floor bedroom (#1)

2nd floor bedroom (#2)   2nd floor bedroom (#3)

2nd floor bedroom (#4)

2nd floor bedroom (#5)

2nd floor bath

The house uses "The Eliminators" to lower the maintenance costs.

Total Rehab costs (still calculating) will be about $70,000.

Costs:	Purchase	$20,000
	2 Settlements	5,000
	Rehab	70,000
	TOTAL:	$95,000

Monthly Numbers:

1) Appraisal $135,000 x 70% Loan to Value = $94,500

2) Cash in house = $500

3) Mortgage 5.75%, 20 years, 5 year balloon, Principal & Interest = $662/month

4) Taxes = $180/month, Insurance = $45/month

5) PITI = $886

6) Rent = $1725 – PITI 886 = 839 Gross Margin

7) GM 839 – Expenses $300 = $539/month

8) Cash on Cash: Cash in $500, Annual Net $6468, Cash on Cash = 1293%

Plus all the other benefits. Not too bad a deal!

DIARY OF A REHAB II

November 1, 2013: Sunset Street had a fire in 2012, at which time the fire department came in with their testosterone-fired tools of destruction and holed the roof, steel cellar door, walls and other parts of the smoke-belching row house. The owners had problems having the insurance company pay the claim. (How unusual!) The house sat lonely and vacant with every rain and snow pouring in from the firemen's entrance points. The municipality grabbed the insurance money and eviscerated the house like a lion takes out an antelope's innards while still warm and moving.

The working folks who had the house in their family for 60 years (background music, tears, crying, screaming It's not fair!) put the house on the MLS for an it-has-to-be-worth-at-least $30,000 as a tax sale approached. I looked at it in mid-2012 but did not make an offer. It was later "sold" and taken off the market in early 2013, but the settlement never materialized and it came back on the market in midyear. I looked at it again, was impressed with its size for a row house—23 feet width—the normal row house is 16 feet. Although the MLS listing had it at 1350 square feet, I measured it at 1850 and pictured 4 bedrooms, 2 full baths, back deck, and yard, and would rent easily.

I offered $8,000. My broker knew the selling broker, who told us that the least they could let it go for, owing taxes and all, was $13,000 or $14,000. I countered at $10,000. They held to $13,000, and I accepted, knowing, as the pictures will attest, the rehab will be extensive, including a new roof and two steel lentils across the front, 1st floor windows where there is an 8" brick opening running down between the windows. Not for the faint of heart.

The rehab will include all mechanicals and I hope to come in at or close to $32 a square foot, or $59,200. As of this date, it is rented for $1350 a month with a move-in date of January 1, 2014.

Front

1st Fl Bedroom

Living Room

Living Room to Dining Room

Kitchen

Full Bath and Washer-Dryer

2nd Fl Front Bedroom Left

2nd Fl Front Bedroom Right

| 2nd Fl Full Bathroom | 2nd Fl Rear Bedroom |

| Basement | Rear |

INTERIM PROGRESS

December 13, 2013:

As you remember, the house was fire/smoke damaged and purchased for $13,000. Here is your interim update of the progress of the rehab.

We were able to buy windows to fit into the current openings. The second floor brickwork needed substantial repair. The roof needed replacement.

The former front porch is now a good-sized 4th bedroom with an entrance door from the living room.

The living room is 23 feet wide and broken into two segments; maybe one for the kids and one for the grownups.

The second half of the living room flows directly into a very large dining room/kitchen.

Huge! More than an eat-in kitchen. Lots of cabinet space. Tiled nicely.

Full tiled bathroom on 1st floor is a nice touch.

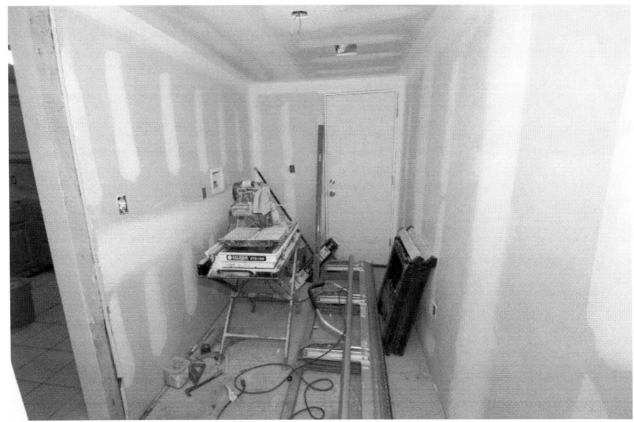

Laundry/Utility Room

2 large 2nd floor bedrooms

Master bedroom. You can get lost traversing this space.

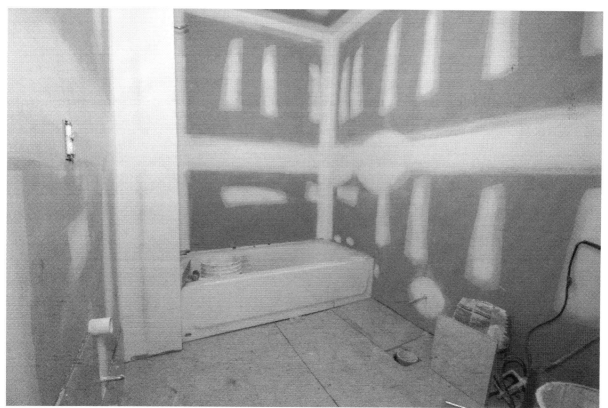
Full bath. Wait 'till you see it when it's finished! Beautiful!

Basement. Mechanicals in. Needs finishing touches

Rear deck and yard. All cleaned up, roof off the deck. Starting to look good!

The house is rented as of January 1, 2014. Can we make it happen? Darn right we will!

JANUARY 2014: IT'S FINISHED!

The fire gutted the house. The fireman put holes in the roof and various other places, the front brick wall was separating in two places, the cellar was still dirt....and I could go on and on. But that's what entrepreneurs are for, aren't we?

This twin is 23' wide; the largest twin I have. We used the window spaces as they were.

The first floor bedroom. New wood gives a nice look. Notice the wall closet. This is our prized 4th bedroom.

Actually two separate living rooms. Lots of space. We refinished the original wood.

Ceramic tile makes a beautiful dining room and flows right into the kitchen.

Lots of cabinet space. A very nice kitchen.

Beautiful full 1st floor bathroom.

Tiled laundry room with door to the rear deck.

The second floor bedrooms with original floors.

Huge master bedroom with new wood.

How would you like to have this bathroom in your home?

Clean, orderly, with everything new, including the cement basement floor.

Took the roof off the deck. Everything is open, neat and clean.

I said we could make it happen, and we DID! January 1, 2014 the tenant moved in with a rental of $1330 a month.

Subscribe to my newsletter at *www.therealestateprofessorbaby.com* and learn how you can receive a FREE copy of THE REHAB BIBLE, my step-by-step instructions on exactly how I rehab houses, including all mechanicals, for about $30 a square foot.

FREE Gifts for you!

Thank you for buying and reading my book! I sincerely hope it helps you achieve your dreams. To further your real estate education, The Real Estate Professor offers you FREE membership to the fastest growing real estate investing newsletter in America! Go to *www.therealestateprofessorbaby.com* and sign up!

Want more free stuff? Go to Amazon and review my book, then go to http://www.therealestateprofessorbaby.com/contact.htm and message me with your choice of one of the following, which you will (again) receive FREE of charge:

- <u>Buy & Rent Foreclosures</u>, my #1 best-selling real estate investing book explaining how in 10 years I have a monthly net of $24K and a net worth of over $4 million.

OR

- <u>The Rehab Bible</u> – My invaluable step-by-step guide on how I do a complete rehab, including mechanicals, for $30 a square foot. If you plan to, or are doing rehabs, this is a MUST HAVE!

"I believe that you can do it!"

Joe Neilson
The Real Estate Professor